T0329008

Cambridge Elements ≡

Elements in Religion and Violence
edited by
James R. Lewis
Wuhan University
Margo Kitts
Hawai'i Pacific University

LONE WOLF RACE WARRIORS AND WHITE GENOCIDE

Mattias Gardell

Uppsala University

CAMBRIDGE
UNIVERSITY PRESS

CAMBRIDGE
UNIVERSITY PRESS

University Printing House, Cambridge CB2 8BS, United Kingdom

One Liberty Plaza, 20th Floor, New York, NY 10006, USA

477 Williamstown Road, Port Melbourne, VIC 3207, Australia

314–321, 3rd Floor, Plot 3, Splendor Forum, Jasola District Centre,
New Delhi – 110025, India

103 Penang Road, #05–06/07, Visioncrest Commercial, Singapore 238467

Cambridge University Press is part of the University of Cambridge.

It furthers the University's mission by disseminating knowledge in the pursuit of
education, learning, and research at the highest international levels of excellence.

www.cambridge.org
Information on this title: www.cambridge.org/9781108711135
DOI: 10.1017/9781108609760

© Mattias Gardell 2021

This publication is in copyright. Subject to statutory exception
and to the provisions of relevant collective licensing agreements,
no reproduction of any part may take place without the written
permission of Cambridge University Press.

First published 2021

A catalogue record for this publication is available from the British Library.

ISBN 978-1-108-71113-5 Paperback
ISSN 2397-9496 (online)
ISSN 2514-3786 (print)

Cambridge University Press has no responsibility for the persistence or accuracy of
URLs for external or third-party internet websites referred to in this publication
and does not guarantee that any content on such websites is, or will remain,
accurate or appropriate.

Lone Wolf Race Warriors and White Genocide

Elements in Religion and Violence

DOI: 10.1017/9781108609760

First published online: June 2021

Mattias Gardell

Uppsala University

Author for correspondence: Mattias Gardell, mattias.gardell@cemfor.uu.se

ABSTRACT: When Brenton Tarrant live-streamed his massacre of fifty-one Muslims in Christchurch, New Zealand, in March 2019, he was but one in a series of lone-acting white men committing violent crime to further the radical white nationalist aim to save the white race from extinction and establish a white ethnostate. From where did white nationalists get the notion of an ongoing white genocide? Why should "resistance" against a perceived invasion of "white" territory be launched by individual "lone wolves" massacring noncombatants they have no prior relation to? How could slaughtering children be construed as a heroic act that a perpetrator wants to broadcast to the world? Based on a unique collection of interviews with lone wolves, their victims, and their supporters, and a close reading of lone wolf, fascist, and radical nationalist material and communication, this Element provides solid answers to these and adjacent questions of importance.

KEYWORDS: lone wolf, fascism, political violence, radical nationalism, violent racism

© Mattias Gardell 2021

ISBNs: 9781108711135 (PB), 9781108609760 (OC)

ISSNs: 2397-9496 (online), 2514-3786 (print)

Contents

1 The Wolves are Coming to Fight

His heart pounded as he hid behind the steel fire door that led from the top floor of the housing complex up to the attic. It was early in the morning, and it would be one of those bright summer days with high blue skies. Birds were singing and he could hear the sound of people waking up in their apartments beneath and around him. Water going through the pipes; people showering, brewing coffee, making breakfast, doors opening, the elevator going up and down. He held the Glock close to his chin, using both hands; barrel pointing upwards, silencer on. Breathing slowly and deeply, listening for one of the doors to any of three apartments of the floor he was at to open. Normally, he never was in this part of the city of Malmö. Thirty-one-year-old Peter Mangs did not know any of the residents, nor did he want to. He only knew they had foreign-sounding surnames, one of them Muslim. He wanted their death, not their friendship.

Mangs heard the sound of a door opening. His heart skipped a beat. "Bingo!" he thought, as he raised his gun between the surprised eyes of the old man in front of him, "the Muslim." Kooros Effatian was a retired customs officer born in Teheran who had fled his country to escape the Islamic Revolution. Mangs did not know that, neither did he ask. To him, the man was Muslim, and today he would die. "The lifeboat is full. We can have no more people in this country," Mangs thought, paraphrasing Finnish eco-fascist Pentti Linkola.[1] The very "survival of the [white] gene-pool is threatened." It was June 13, 2003, and the world would never be the same again. He was "programmed to solve all problems." Mangs squeezed the trigger. "Give war a chance."[2]

Dressed as a police officer, thirty-three-year-old Anders Behring Breivik got help carrying off his heavy bags, loaded with guns and ammo, as the ferry landed at Utøya island in idyllic Lake Tyri, northwest of Oslo. One and a half hours earlier, Breivik had detonated a homemade bomb at the government headquarters in downtown Oslo, killing eight people and wounding 209. He now killed the camp organizer and the

---

[1] Mangs, Interview, June 17, 2014; Linkola, 2011.

[2] Mangs, *German Philosophy*, n.d.

security guard on the wharf and walked toward the old main house on the island. He summoned the young adults assembled there for the yearly Labor Youth Utøya Summer Camp; "I came here to protect you." As the boys and girls flocked around him, Breivik brought out his Ruger Mini-14 and Glock 34 and began shooting the youngsters, one by one, systematically, smiling, enjoying himself. Some teenagers ran off; others froze in panic, unable to move even when the killer stopped to reload his guns. Breivik recalls walking around the island, looking for kids hiding in the woods, behind rocks, down by the shores, or throwing themselves in the water, all the while listening to "Lux Aeterna" by Clint Mansell on his iPod, the evocative violin-led hymn played during the battle scenes in *Lord of the Rings: The Two Towers*. It took an hour and a half. He killed sixty-nine youths that summer day, July 22, 2011, and wounded forty-one, including eighteen who were hospitalized in critical condition. Breivik was proud of himself. His only regret was that he did not kill more traitors to stop the ongoing genocide on the "indigenous (white) peoples of Europe," as explained in his *2083: A Declaration of European Independence*, which he had mailed to select recipients earlier that morning.[3]

"Well lads," twenty-eight-year-old Brenton Tarrant wrote on 8chan's "pol" board, where a community of alt-right people gather, on March 15, 2019, "it's time to stop shitposting and time to make a real-life effort post. I will carry out an attack against the invaders, and will even live stream the attack via Facebook. The Facebook link is below, by the time you read this I should be going live."[4] He mounted a camera on his helmet and drove down to the local Christchurch mosque to the tones of a Serbian song celebrating genocide on Muslims: "The wolves are coming to fight."[5] Cheering spectators sitting by their computers across the world followed Tarrant into the mosque from the perspective of a first-person-shooter video game, seeing the enlarged barrels of the shotgun and the people encountered and shot in the rooms and hallways of the building. Tarrant took fifty-one lives and wounded another fifty-six that day – men, women, and children.

---

[3] Breivik, Interview, June 19, 2014; Breivik, 2011, pp. 967, 1033f, 1121, 1130, 1353f.
[4] Tarrant, Facebook Live stream, 2019b. [5] Tarrant, Facebook Live stream, 2019b.

Malmö, Sweden, 2003; Oslo, Norway, 2011; Christchurch, New Zealand, 2019. Three armed white men killing people whose names they did not know, yet who they defined as invaders, traitors, polluters. All three saw themselves as heroes risking their lives in defense of their nation, although their targets were all unarmed civilians. The neighbors, friends, and colleagues of Mangs, Breivik, and Tarrant were stupefied when hearing the news. They had found them polite and tidy, never having expressed extremist views. The investigations showed they all had adopted the same tactics described in white nationalist literature and known as *leaderless resistance*, and had learned to avoid advance detection by melting into the general population. Though they had never met, they saw themselves as part of the same "resistance," sharing tactics, political views, references, myths, and visions. "Lone" perpetrators of this kind are not "alone" other than operationally.

Such performative acts of weaponized whiteness do not only target the individuals they happen to kill, but the communities of racialized others their victims were forced to represent by being killed. None of the killers knew their victims personally. They knew only what their victims represented to them: worthless life that had to die for valuable life to prosper. The murders were political, meant to amplify existing tensions in society, to ignite the apocalyptic race war through which the white nation would be born anew.

While years apart, the killings in Malmö, Oslo, and Christchurch were not isolated, but part of a series of lethal assaults similar in style and motivation perpetrated across the global North. In fact, this kind of political violence has been sufficiently commonplace to award the individual racist attacker their own epithet within the milieu of white radical nationalism: "lone wolf", a metaphor loaded with romantic notions of the potency and lethality of the free-roaming outcast, suiting the hero politics idealized in the milieu.

It has become part of the pattern for perpetrators of lone wolf violence to explain their cause in writings and/or videoclips.[6] Breivik saw July 22, 2011 as a "marketing operation" for his 1,571-page *2083* manifesto.[7] Similarly,

---

[6] Nilsson, forthcoming, 2021. [7] Breivik, 2011, p. 16.

Tarrant posted his own manifesto, *The Great Replacement*, minutes before the attack, a call to arms to stop the alleged genocide of white people worldwide.

Like Breivik, Tarrant calculated that the more shocking and appalling his violent attack, the greater the attention he would receive. Thus, in the section of *The Great Replacement* in which he interviews himself – another detail he took from Breivik – Tarrant asks himself, "Children are always innocent, do you not think you are a monster for killing an innocent?" "No," he responds. "Children of invaders do not stay children, they become adults and reproduce, creating more invaders to replace your people." In Tarrant's mind, slaying children becomes the noble thing to do. "Any invader you kill, of any age, is one less enemy your children will have to face. Would you rather do the killing, or leave it to your children?"[8]

How did we get here? From where did white nationalists get the notion of an ongoing white genocide happening on their watch? How did they come to the conclusion that "resistance" against a perceived invasion and occupation of "white" territory should be launched by individual "lone wolves" performing ghastly massacres on noncombatants with whom they had no prior relation? How come slaughtering innocent children is construed as a heroic act that a perpetrator wants to broadcast to the world?

The answers will be sought by following the trail of the lone wolf in the political landscape of white nationalism. In so doing, I will proceed from the approach of "methodological empathy," as developed by Roger Griffin within the field of Fascism Studies.[9] In seeking to understand a Peter Mangs, an Anders Behring Breivik, or a Brenton Tarrant, it is not enough to run a LexisNexis search or to rely on intelligence reports, court proceedings, the accounts of their victims, or assessments by reporters and political opponents. To understand fascists, it is necessary to engage with them and the material they produce and are inspired by.

This Element builds on four categories of material: first, ethnographic material produced during fieldwork among white nationalists, interviews with lone wolves, including Peter Mangs and Anders Behring Breivik, and conversations with people who see their deeds as heroic; second, material

---

[8] Tarrant, 2019a, p. 22.   [9] Griffin, 2008.

produced by lone wolves themselves, including their manifestos, books, statements, social media postings, live streams, and films, and the literature and people they refer to and were inspired by; third, court proceedings, police investigations, and testimonies; finally, secondary sources, including media reports and previous studies of white nationalism, fascism, and political violence.

Contested Concepts

Words are not innocent. The concepts we use open up the way we think about certain issues, and simultaneously close or obscure other ways of understanding that which we have before us. In what follows, I will discuss why and how I use certain key concepts in this Element: nation/nationalism/radical nationalism, fascism, accelerationism, and ethnopluralism.

The concept of "radical nationalism" is used to name a *political landscape* that encompasses a wide variety of overlapping and not infrequently competing political traditions, including national socialism, populist nativism, alt-right, deep right, fascism, eco-fascism, occult fascism, identitarianism, radical traditionalism, tribal socialism, and national bolshevism, all of which are open to different and instable interpretations that may spur further schismatic divisions.

While most radical nationalist movements tend to be small and transitory, the landscape itself is still there, kept alive by publications, political philosophies, artworks, music, and by the narratives and legends of triumph, challenges, and grievances, which revolve around the polyvalent notions of nation, tradition, and race.

Radical nationalist leaders frequently lay emphasis on the differences between their respective parties, philosophies, and approaches, such as highlighting the contrasts between competing national socialist parties, the distinctions between radical traditionalism and national bolshevism, and the dissimilarities between those who by principle or tactics participate in parliamentary elections and those who do not.

Irrespective of how important these distinctions are to diehards, who may even brand those of other factions traitors, scores of rank-and-file tour the landscape to visit its various sites, not least online; people in leading positions suddenly break off to form new groups or switch alliances, and most sympathizers will probably spend most of their time unorganized, while generally sympathetic to important parts of the white nationalist landscape, if not of everything that goes on.

The *nations* for which they fight are not necessarily the same as the nations of the actually existing nation-states. A Swedish radical nationalist may fight to save a "nation" defined as Swedish and/or Nordic, European, Western, and White, or engage in a separatist project to carve out a piece of contemporary Sweden (e.g., Scania, Jämtland, Norrland) as an independent nation. While centering on the particular nation they hold uniquely theirs, radical nationalists may recognize, celebrate, and support each other across national borders, as illustrated by Narendra Modi and Donald Trump, Viktor Orbán and Benjamin Netanyahu, publicly embracing each other and forging transnational links of nationalist solidarity.

A nation may be founded on blood, territory, creed, divine intervention, or a combination thereof, but is always exclusionary, albeit to some extent open to accept outsiders under certain conditions. To a radical nationalist, the nation is of overarching importance, the very "root" of human existence. A human without a nation is a rootless being fleeting aimlessly in a sea of meaninglessness.

In nationalist imagination, a nation is a transhistoric entity of organic solidarity with a specific essence that nationalists hold uniquely theirs. More than the sum of its inherent qualities, the nation is something that nationalists "believe in" and bestow with certain "rights," such as the rights of autonomy, prosperity, and self-determination in a territory of its own, typically called its "home" – objectives a radical nationalist is obliged to fight, kill, and die for.

A "nation" is an "imagined community," involving feelings of solidarity with people of the same nation, despite the fact that we will never meet or know more than a fraction of those compatriots during our lifetime.[10] The fact that we actually may identify with people who to us are anonymous and who may be living in places we have never heard of, or those who are dead or yet unborn, as long as they "belong" to the same "nation," tells us not to

[10] Andersen, 1991.

equate "imagined" with "unreal." Nationalists produce the imagined nation by projecting it back into legendary or mythological time, often presented as a "golden age" of national greatness. "Born" during the golden age, the particular nation is endowed with certain inherent qualities, a personal history, and a "destiny" to be fulfilled in a glorious future if the current crisis nationalists typically thinks the nation suffers from is overcome.

Other terms used in the literature to connote what is here named radical nationalism include the "far right," the "radical right," "rightwing extremism," the "extreme right," and "rightwing radicalism." Some scholars use these terms interchangeably; others seek to integrate them as distinct types in a typology. However, there is no consensus on which groups should be classified, how, and by which criteria. Is the far right more extreme than the radical or vice versa?

The confusion may be partly explained by the fact that the term *radical right* is American in origin, while *rightwing extremism* is European. The first was coined by scholars exploring McCarthyism and the anti-communist "crusades" of the 1950s; the second was used to understand postwar fascism and national socialism in Europe.[11] Both concepts expanded to include nativism and violent racism – such as the Ku Klux Klan in the USA, and militant anti-immigrant groups in Europe – crossed the Atlantic, and collided with each other in various ways.

Miroslav Mareš and Tore Bjørgo draw a distinction between the "extreme" and the "radical" right on the grounds that the former "accept or even condone violence,"[12] and Jens Rydgren argues that "rightwing extremism" is opposed to democracy, while the "radical right wing" is not necessarily so.[13] In this article, these positions are part of the radical nationalist landscape, and the questions of violence and democracy are but a few of several issues debated in terms of principles, instruments, tactics, and timing.

Empirically, there is not much to justify the rightwing label (whether "extreme" or "radical"), as the discourses and agendas of the parties,

---

[11] Kaplan & Weinberg, 1998. [12] Bjørgo & Mareš, 2019.
[13] Rydgren, 2018; Cas Mudde, 2016, counted twenty-six different scholarly definitions of "rightwing extremism," with fifty-eight different features.

movements, and lead voices in the landscape feature elements of both the right (e.g., tradition, nation, law and order, gender essentialism, moral conservatism) and the left (e.g., [white] workers' rights, women's rights, elderly people's rights, environmental concerns). Radical nationalism is typically anti-capitalist *and* anti-communist, as seen in its slogan "neither left, nor right, but forward."

An important constellation in the landscape is *fascism*, a term I use in its generic sense as defined by Roger Griffin to connote a revolutionary form of radical nationalism centred on a mythic core of national rebirth.[14] "Myth" is used here in the tradition of the history of religions, where the concept signifies narratives, stories, and claims that are considered to convey truth in a meaningful way. To a fascist, the nation's mythic origins and historical greatness are unquestionable, and the vision of national rebirth is something that can and should be realized.

Radical nationalism is the broader term. Every fascist is per definition a radical nationalist, but not every radical nationalist is a fascist. Radical nationalism and fascism both seek to return the nation to its former glory, to "Make the Nation Great Again," as the slogan goes. A non-fascist radical nationalist may believe that it is possible to achieve this aim by reformist strategies only: put the nation first, build a wall, restrict immigration, and the like. To a fascist radical nationalist, nothing but systemic change will do; only revolution will secure the rebirth of the nation.

History has seen a variety of different fascisms developing in various times and places. Japanese fascism is not exactly the same as Romanian fascism, and the Italian fascism of the 2020s is not exactly the same as the Italian fascism of the 1920s. Like any other political philosophy, fascism transforms with time and changing contexts.

Obviously, fascism received a "knock-out blow" at the end of the Second World War and has since sought to overcome its "toxic legacies" and its wholescale discrediting in public opinion by regrouping, reorganizing, revising, reformulating, refashioning, and rebranding itself, aiming to creating for itself "another name, another face." As French fascist theorist Maurice Bardèche argued already in 1961: "With the form of a child we do

[14]   Griffin, 1992; 2018.

not recognize and the head of a young Medusa, the Order of Sparta will be reborn."[15]

Fascism with a new face is sometimes labeled "neo-fascism." However, what is considered "recent" is unstable and dependent on time. The articulations of fascism that were called "new" in the 1960s or 1980s may seem dated in the 2020s. That problem can hardly be solved by pasting on new prefixes as time goes by, which invite us to study "new neo-fascism," "newer new neo-fascism," and "really, really new neo-fascism." To see fascism as a generic term is to acknowledge that fascism, much like socialism, liberalism, and conservatism, changes according to changing contexts and conditions.

While fascism is a revolutionary form of radical nationalism, there is no uniform fascist theory on how the revolution will be accomplished. Important to our purpose is a theory sometimes named *accelerationism*, which seeks to amplify the contradictions inherent to the system to see it destroy itself. "Stability and comfort are the enemies of revolutionary change," Tarrant wrote, insisting that fascists should not favor policies that make life better for white people, but should instead aim at "supporting, attacking, vilifying, radicalizing and exaggerating all societal conflicts."[16]

According to accelerationist fascism, the nation cannot be reborn or saved by seizing power and implementing policies to regain national greatness, in the manner Hitler and Mussolini once tried (and in which they ultimately failed). We are past the point of no return. To be born anew, the nation must first die. Total war will pave the way for national rebirth. The cleansing fire will not only consume the nation's foes but the vast majority of ordinary white folks, who have proven their worthlessness by allowing the situation to come this far. "Strong men do not get ethnically replaced," Tarrant wrote. "Weak men have created this situation and strong men are needed to fix it."[17]

There is no way back to the Golden Age of national greatness; history cannot go backwards, only forwards, irrespective of whether time is linear or cyclic. Hence, the only meaningful thing a fascist may do is to accelerate the inevitable, hasten the onslaught of the approaching Ragnarök, and build

---

[15] Griffin, 2017. [16] Tarrant, 2019a, p. 66. [17] Tarrant, 2019a, p. 30.

the new on the ruins of the old. Apocalyptic war will separate the wheat from the chaff and galvanize the seeds of the becoming New Man who will make up the nation that will arise anew out of the ashes of total destruction.

Increasingly important to white nationalism is *ethnopluralism*, a theory of racial difference and national belonging popularized in the European "new right" and prevalent in contemporary identitarian and alt-right discourse.[18] Ethnopluralism connotes the idea that mankind may be divided into a mosaic of demarcated "varieties" (to use Carl Linnaeus' word), named races, cultures, religions, or ethnicities, each bestowed with an inherited essence and certain unique features. Linking race and space, blood and soil, each variety is held to belong in a certain place of origin, called its home, and those who do not belong anywhere, such as the Roma, constitute a problem. As long as each kind stay in their proper place, they are considered pure, and to some extent valuable, at least in theory. However, if they move from their assigned place, they become out-of-place and thereby impure and threatening, according to the logic Mary Douglas theorized in *Purity and Danger*.[19] Should people associated with a particular variety mix, live with, and crossbreed with people of another variety, then disharmony, unhappiness, and disorder will follow. Imperialism is therefore disastrous, and so is colonialism – unless the settler-colony exterminates all but its own kind from the conquered territory.

As the theory of "white supremacy" developed to legitimize white rule over nonwhite people in the colony, post-colony, and empire, it has lost ground in the landscape of white nationalism, in which separatism and "the right to differ" rather than colonialism and globalism sets the tone. Racial separatist Richard McCulloch rejects white supremacy as "immoral" as it violates the rights of other races by subjugating and exploiting them. All races have "the right to exist" as distinct forms of life, "free from domination, control or interference by other races."[20]

---

[18] Bar-On, 2001; 2014; McCulloch, *The Racial Compact: A Call for Racial Rights, Preservation, and Independence*, n.d.

[19] Douglas, 1966.

[20] McCulloch, *The Racial Compact: A Call for Racial Rights, Preservation, and Independence*, n.d.

While opposed in theory, ethnopluralism and white supremacy may in practice be combined, as evidenced by apartheid, which is racial difference within a supremacist frame. Thus, ethnopluralism strives for homogeneity, ethnocracy, and cultural hegemony in "its own" territorial space, while opposing multiculturalism and egalitarianism as forms of genocide.[21]

Brenton Tarrant was all of the above: a white radical nationalist and ethnopluralist who subscribed to the accelerationist fascist theory of using violence to increase the contradictions, antagonisms, and animosities inherent to the system he hoped to see explode in violent upheaval – a total destruction out of which the white nation he fought for would rise as the mythical phoenix out of the ashes. Other lone wolves before and after did not necessarily share all the same traits and positions, but all were white nationalists and most often fascist, and all saw violence as the primary means to secure a glorious future for the white nation and their own heroic status in the Aryan hall of fame.

2 What are Lone Wolf Tactics?

The term "lone wolf" is a metaphor that began to be used by white radical nationalists in the 1970s to connote unorganized individuals who committed violent crime to further white racist/white nationalist aims. In the 1980s and 1990s, radical nationalist thinkers, including James Mason, Louis Beam, and David Lane, incorporated lone wolf violence as part of decentralized tactics often, though not exclusively, named "leaderless resistance."

Contemplating the fact that white racist organizations had not been able to protect white people from successively losing the powers and privileges attached to whiteness thereto protected by American law and custom, Mason, Beam and Lane concluded that not only were these organizations – the Ku Klux Klan(s) included – dysfunctional, impotent and weak, but also far too visible and easy to monitor, infiltrate, and neutralize. While the white "resistance" still needed public organizations and leaders for propaganda and education, armed resistance should be decentralized and leaderless. White nationalist leaders should issue generalized calls to arms, but

[21] Griffin, 2014, p. 51.

give no direct orders, and have no advance knowledge of who was planning what. The more random and unpredictable the violence, the better. Perpetrators would themselves be responsible for planning, financing, and implementing their violence, as well as acquiring relevant resources and skills. To go under the radar, a would-be perpetrator should shun white nationalist organizations and avoid revealing his or her political views or bragging about what he or she would do. The perpetrator would risk his or her life or freedom but be included as a hero in the white nationalist hall of fame. To leaders, such tactics were cost-effective. A perpetrator disconnected to organized racism could do the movement no harm and would have no direct information about white nationalist organizations and their leaders to reveal to the police.[22]

Initially, "lone wolf" was used interchangeably with alternative metaphors such as "lone eagle," "lone warrior," and "one-man army," but eventually became the term that stuck.[23] Wolves and eagles are impressive predators, and "good to think with" in myths and sagas. In modern American culture, the lone eagle symbolizes the spirit of freedom and sovereign majesty, but as the bald eagle is also the emblem of the United States, the eagle metaphor became increasingly tainted for radical white nationalists who came to see the government as their enemy. The lone wolf had no such connotations in popular white American culture. Seen as free, feared, and lethal, the lone wolf symbolized the outlaw and was associated with the wilderness, frontier culture, outlaw bikers, and the legendary gunmen of the Wild, Wild West. The lone wolf is an outcast, yet a hero, lyricized in numerous Hollywood productions as the lone avenger, the vigilante, Zorro, the lone ranger – almost always white, male, and often rich, a born aristocrat, yet against the establishment; a true American hero.

The fact that the lone wolf was adopted by fascists as an embodiment of heroic white masculinity alongside the Viking, the berserker, the Spartan, and the Crusader knight is hardly surprising. Fascism travels in myth and legend, and the *lone wolf* does its work by appealing to white radical nationalist warrior dreams and alpha-male fantasies.

---

[22] Mason, 1992d; Beam, 1983. [23] Mason, 1981c; Warthan, "Terrorism," n.d.

Lone Wolves, Stray Dogs, Lone Rats, Lone Wolf Packs, Lone Actors

As the number of murders, bombings, and arson attacks committed by individual white radical nationalists increased during the 1980s and 1990s, the leaderless lone wolf tactics began to attract attention from scholars and true-crime authors.

The first researcher to award the lone wolf phenomenon scholarly attention was Jeffrey Kaplan, a student of religion, apocalypticism, and the American "radical right" who actually talks to people in the milieus of observation and is sensitive to what is going on. In a 1997 article, Kaplan saw leaderless resistance as a "mark of despair" disseminated to the "far right faithful" to make a virtue of the milieu's weakness, and used the term "lone wolf" to connote instances where "an individual, or a very small, highly cohesive group, engage in acts of anti-state violence independent of any movement, leader or network of support."[24] In a 1998 comparative study of the religious dimensions of white and black nationalism in the United States, I conducted several interviews with American fascist exponents of lone wolf tactics, and returned to the subject as one out of many during an extended fieldwork of white separatism and the pagan revival published in 2003.[25]

By the turn of the millennium, incidents of white fascist violence were recurrently directed against racialized and sexual minorities as well as government officials and buildings. The 1990s had seen the rise of militias, sovereign citizens, and a series of armed standoffs with white racist communities. There were fears of black helicopters, the New World Order, hidden federal concentration camps, and widespread white anxiety over the devaluation of white heterosexual masculinity, aptly captured in *Falling Down*. Calls for white resistance were disseminated at gun shows, on talk radio, and over the worldwide web, at a time when the proportion of American households with computers and Internet rose from less than 20 to around 50 percent in a decade. "The overwhelming majority of extremist groups in the United States have

---

[24] Kaplan, 1997a; cf. forthcoming. [25] Gardell, 1998a; 2003.

adopted a fragmented, leaderless structure where individuals or small groups act with autonomy," the FBI wrote in an assessment of the threat of domestic terrorism predominantly coming from white nationalist milieus for whom the "battle of Armageddon is interpreted as a race war." "Extremists of this sort are extremely difficult to identify until after an incident has occurred."[26]

Then came September 11. While fascism remained the most significant threat of domestic terrorism in the US, with white nationalists committing some three-quarters of all political assaults resulting in death, resources and attention were, under the War on Terror, largely reallocated to the threat of "Islamic terrorism." While American Muslim suspects could be charged for committing acts of terrorism, white nationalists suspected for committing "domestic terrorism" could not be charged accordingly as there is no federal statute for domestic terrorism.[27]

As the number of terrorism incidents rose from a record low of 1,800 (in the year of 2000) to a record high of 17,000 (in 2017) under the (quite counterproductive) War on Terror,[28] so too did the number of assaults committed by unorganized Islamists in the West. According to Sara Teich, there were four attacks or attempted attacks by "Islamic extremists" acting alone between 1990 and 1999. During the first decade of the

---

[26] FBI, 1999. [27] Kamali, 2021; US Government Accountability Office, 2017.

[28] Growing exponentially was also Terrorism Studies, a field that had emerged during the 1970s and was primarily devoted to "red terror," but which had found the War on Terror a haven of career opportunities, with an estimated publication rate of one book every six hours. Per-Erik Nilsson has found much of mainstream Terrorism Studies to be an interreferential milieu of experts not always excelling in methodological skills and critical thinking, and with compromisingly close ties to state interests. Despite all contrary evidence, "terrorism" became regarded as something only non-state actors do. This fact is reflected in the cited statistics by the Global Terrorism Database that define terrorism as "violence by a non-state actor to attain a political, economic, religious, or social goal through fear, coercion, or intimidation" (Nilsson, 2018; Global Terrorism Database, "Defining Terrorism," n.d.).

War on Terror, there was a ten-time increase to forty incidents by lone actors motivated by "general Al-Qaeda ideology or a thirst for jihad."[29]

Teich referred to these "thirsty" individuals as Islamic "lone wolves," and thereby took a side in a scholarly debate on terminology that had begun a few years earlier and continues to this day. Could scholars use a term developed by fascists? Could it be applied to actors of other political milieus? More specifically, could a fascist metaphor used to hail unorganized individuals who commit violent assault to further a fascist goal be applied to unorganized individuals who commit violent crime to advance the aims of al-Qaida or the Islamic State?

In a study of "Islamic terrorism" in the US since September 11, Bryan Jenkins, senior advisor at the RAND Corporation, dismissed the term completely. To Jenkins, lone wolf was a "romanticizing term that suggests a cunning and deadly predator. A few of those recorded here display this kind of lethal determination, but others, while still dangerous, skulk about, sniffing at violence, vocally aggressive but skittish without backup. 'Stray dogs,' not lone wolves, more accurately describes their behavior."[30] FBI Director James Comey agreed, arguing that the term lone wolf conveys a "sense of dignity" these perpetrators do not deserve, suggesting "lone rats" as better capturing lost souls "emerging from their basement" to "engage in jihad."[31] Echoing Jenkins, Bart Schuurman et al. similarly reject lone wolf as a "sensationalist term that originated with American right-wing extremists" and that implies a "high level of cunning and lethality that rarely is found among these individuals."[32]

Lone wolves, stray dogs, lone rats – are all emotionally laden concepts of awe or contempt that illustrate the importance of the affective dimension of these political landscapes in which hero politics is such an outstanding feature. Politics, like man, is not only driven by reason and rational choice, but also by desire, passion, visons, dreams, and longings. While "lone wolf" is used by white nationalists to celebrate their own heroes, and thus may feed the warrior dreams of new generations of

---

[29] Teich, 2013. [30] Jenkins, 2011.
[31] "FBI Director on Threat of ISIS, Cybercrime," 2014.
[32] Schuurman et al., 2019.

fascists, the term rarely enters al-Qaida or Islamic State publications, except when quoting Western terrorism studies and government experts.[33]

In its own inspirational calls to potential sympathizers in the West, al-Qaida typically evokes romanticized imagery in other terms, as exemplified by the invitation "To the Knights of the Lone Jihad": "You are the knight who strikes the enemy's heart, penetrating his armor, exposing his vulnerabilities. You are the David who cuts down the Goliath. This unique heroic act can only by performed by you, with steadfast determination, unfaltering courage, and rock-solid resolution. Few are selected by Allah for this purpose."[34]

Other terms used by al-Qaida and the Islamic State to hail their own heroes include "martyrs," "servants," or "soldiers" of God. When reference is made to the animal kingdom, *lions*, not wolves, seem to be the image of preference to signify bravery, strength, and valor. "You have your B52s, your Apaches, your Abrams, and your Cruise missiles and we have small arms and simple Improvised Explosive Devices, but we have men who are dedicated and sincere, with hearts of lions," wrote Anwar al-Awlaki in an article hailing Nidal Hasan,[35] a US Army major and psychiatrist who fatally shot thirteen and wounded thirty-two military personnel at the Ford Hood Army Post in Killeen, Texas on November 5, 2009.

Similarly, the Islamic State calls its volunteer fighters "lions" and its young recruits "lion cubs," and urges its sympathizers in the West to "follow the example of the lions who have preceded them by striking the Crusader citizens and interests wherever they are found in the West."[36]

Thus, both al-Qaida and the Islamic State literally *lionize* their individual heroes who risk their lives by bringing the War of Terror back to the land of its instigation and hope to inspire successors by distributing online handbooks with practical advice on how to build bombs and turn cars and kitchen tools into weapons.[37] Had this Element been about unorganized

---

[33] See, for example, "Inspire Reactions," 2015.

[34] "To the Knights of the Lone Jihad," 2013. [35] al-Awlaki, 2010.

[36] "A Message from East Africa," 2016; "Wilāyat Ar-Raqqah – Ramadān 26," 2014.

[37] *Lone Mujahid Pocketbook*, 2013; *How to Survive in the West: A Mujahid Guide*, 2015.

sympathizers to al-Qaida or the Islamic State who commit violent crime to further a militant Islamist aim, I would not have called them lone wolves but "lions" and "martyrs" when discussing my findings from the perspective of methodological empathy.

To avoid romanticizing terms originating within the milieus of study, scholars such as Schuurman et al. call for a "dispassionate empirical research" and suggest the more prosaic term "lone actor."[38] Other scholars, including Ramón Spaaij and Mark S. Hamm, disagree. "Even if the term 'lone wolf terrorism' does glamorize the loner, there is no evidence that this has impeded problem-solving capabilities." Not only is the term already "generally accepted," but it remains a "useful analytical tool" because it captures the "uniqueness of this specific type of ideologically motivated violence."[39]

To Hamm and Spaaij it is not lone wolves' ideological motivation but the very status of the "loner" that makes lone wolves unique, poorly understood, and unpredictable. However, that very feature does not distinguish "lone wolf" from "lone actor." Both terms signify unorganized individuals who receive no training, finances, or assistance from any network, group, or organization but are left to secure the arms, equipment, safe houses, and escape routes on their own – not the easiest thing to do on your free time, without sponsors. Moreover, should the lone wolf/lone actor get second thoughts about the righteousness of randomly killing people in a mosque, synagogue, youth camp, or school, he or she is left to overcome the qualms on his or her own. Unsurprisingly, then, these assaults are still relatively rare, and often fail to turn out as planned.

Most, though not all, scholars seeking to understand lone wolf/lone actor tactics rarely interact with or even meet the people they write about, spending more time in their offices and at conferences than in the political landscape they seek to understand. Among these armchair scholars, a segment are building databases and computing their entries. The art of defining here determines the value of that which counts, and determines what is countable. To which digit should a complex event be reduced? The definition of lone wolf suggested by Kaplan, as an individual or a very small

---

[38] Schuurman et al., 2019. [39] Hamm & Spaaij, 2017, p. 6f; cf. Michael, 2012.

group engaged in anti-state violence independent of outside support, becomes too imprecise to serve this end. Is a lone wolf an individual and/or a group? How small is a very small group? What does independent mean in a milieu responding to generalized calls to arms? To calculate, numbers are needed, not the ambiguities of life. What is a zero (0) and what is a one (1)?

To Ramón Spaaij and Mark S. Hamm, lone wolves per definition act "totally alone"; there is no second party. This excludes widely renowned cases, including the 1995 Oklahoma City bombing; Timothy McVeigh had an accomplice, Terry Nichols, who allegedly aided him in building the fuel-and-ammonium-nitrate-fertilizer bomb and arranged for a car, but who was at his Kansas farm, hundreds of miles away from Oklahoma City, on the day of the attack.[40]

Excluding acts by pairs would be inaccurate, according to Paul Gill et al., who included the Oklahoma City bombing in a comparative five-case study of "lone actor terrorism."[41] In a later study, Gill and his teammates built a lone actor terrorism database that included "isolated dyads" and "isolated individuals" in the data gathered. When discussing their findings in *Bombing Alone* and elsewhere, Gill et al. admit that individuals operating in pairs cannot "technically" be considered "lone" actors. Yet, they argue, dyads should be included as: (1) the analysis focuses on "terrorists" who "are not members of terrorist groups"; (2) case reviews show that dyads are often formed when one individual recruits another for an attack; and (3) their inclusion adds to the sample size, which makes inferential statistics more applicable.[42]

More is more, and Raffaello Pantucci expands the term lone wolf to "lone wolf packs" when referring to small isolated groups pursuing political goals but operating without direction from, or formal connection with, an organization or network. "The principle behind the Lone Wolf Pack is one that is similar to the Lone Wolves," Pantucci argues, "except rather than there being a single individual who becomes ideologically motivated; it is

---

[40] Hamm & Spaaij, 2017, pp. 5, 23, 30, 33; Spaaij, 2012. [41] Gill et al., 2012.
[42] Gill et al., 2014; cf. Gill, 2016.

a group of individuals who self-radicalise."[43] How large a wolf pack can be before it turns into a group or movement remains unclear.

A definitional workshop organized by the Countering Lone-Actor Terrorism (CLAT) project basically returned to Kaplan's original definition by applying the term to a single perpetrator working within a small autonomous cell; however, it set a limit for participants to three, thereby allowing for a definition of "lone actor" to include a dyad or triad of people as long as they operated without direction from a wider network or outside leadership.[44]

In this Element, the term "lone wolf" will not be used as an analytical concept, but as a metaphor utilized by white radical nationalists to signify a category of Aryan Heroes: unorganized individuals who without orders or assistance commit or plans to commit violent crime(s) to further a white radical nationalist objective. Hence, whether these individuals ask a friend to give them a hand is of secondary importance as long as they are understood as lone wolves by fellow white nationalists and are awarded heroic status accordingly.

Same, Same, but Different

Lone actors are not unique to the white radical nationalist milieu. Currents within at least four political milieus have at some point elevated individual acts of illegal violence as celebrated parts of a decentralized resistance:

1) insurrectionary anarchism
2) white radical nationalism
3) antiabortionism
4) militant Islamism

Of course, all four are political milieus in which not everyone agrees with everyone else. This includes opinions about lone actor violence that have never been universally approved within the milieus from which they spring – a fact that has not always been noted in research. In the literature on lone actor political violence, these four distinct political milieus have

---

[43] Pantucci, 2011, pp. 8, 24.
[44] Bakker & de Roy van Zuijdewijn, 2014; Ellis et al., 2016a; 2016b.

recurrently been treated *as if* they were parts of the same history, as if they were interconnected through intellectual, political, ethical, and/or personal links, and as if the milieus that adopted the tactics later in time were inspired by the milieu(s) that previously developed the tactics.

It has become increasingly customary to begin a study of "lone wolf terrorism" with the anarchist milieu in Europe, Russia, and North America at the turn of the previous century, a period historian Richard Bach Jensen calls "the classic age of lone wolf or leaderless terrorism," 1878–1934.[45] Thereafter, these studies typically jump to the 1980s or 1990s, and the white-power-oriented lone wolves, and proceed to al-Qaida and the Islamic State in the twenty-first century. If the time gap of 50, 80, or 100 years is at all discussed, it tends to be glossed over by inserting some concept that obscures rather than clarifies what kind of alleged connection there is. Let me illustrate.

"Lone wolf terrorism," sociologist Rodger Bates claims, "long employed by extremist movements," owes "part of its origins" to "the writings of Mikhail Bakunin and Sergey Nechayev," who "championed the concept of 'propaganda by deed' in the mid-19th century", which now has been "resurrected by radical right-wing extremists, Islamic jihadists, and others."[46] Of course, to claim that something has been employed for a long time implies a certain continuity, while resurrection implies that something died out only to be revived again. In both cases, the reader is left with the impression that there somehow is a link between mid-nineteenth-century anarchism and "right-wing" and "Islamic" extremism of today – a claim Bates does not substantiate.

Similarly, when Jensen refers to the hundreds of violent deeds, including spectacular assassinations of heads of state, committed by anarchists operating alone or in small cells at the turn of the twentieth century as the "classic age of lone wolf terrorism,"[47] the practices and theories of the anarchist insurrectionists are bestowed iconic status and treated as if they were the starting point in an interreferential system of "lone wolf" practitioners. Referring to these anarchists as "lone wolf classics" is to say that the white fascist, al-Qaida, and Islamic State thinkers and milieus that later

[45] Jensen, 2014; 2015. [46] Bates, 2012. [47] Jensen, 2014.

developed their lone wolf and lone martyr tactics did so with reference to Bakunin, Enrico Malatesta, Carlo Cafiero, Emilio Covelli, Alexander Berkman, or any of the other anarchists who favored the tactics of decentralized direct action and propaganda by deed.

However, while the anarchist bombing campaigns and the assassinations of the presidents of France and the USA, the prime minister of Spain, the king of Italy, and the empress of Austria and queen of Hungary[48] may have shaken the world at the turn of the previous century and scared US President Theodore Roosevelt into signing the Anarchist Exclusion Act of 1903,[49] these events seem to have gone unnoticed by white radical nationalists and al-Qaida and Islamic State thinkers of today.

A careful review of the writings and speeches of the white fascist ideologues who introduced lone wolf and leaderless resistance tactics in the white power milieu demonstrate that they did *not* refer to the anarchist insurrectionists of the nineteenth and early twentieth centuries, but were in fact influenced by *other* political thinkers and traditions. If white fascist literature mentions anarchists, they are typically referred to as *political enemies*, not role models. After all, fascists are generally aware that anarchists tend to be anti-fascist.

The closest to an exception I have been able to find is in the writings of the national socialist ideologue James Mason, who actually mentions Mikhail Bakunin in his *Siege* magazine five times: twice in 1980, once in 1985, and twice in an undated text. Mason was an early advocate for lone wolf political violence and accelerationist fascism. To build his case for leaderless terror, it would have been logical for Mason to have looked at Bakunin's writings on spontaneous violence, propaganda by deed, and the lust of destruction. But no. Mason approvingly cites Bakunin's thought that a revolutionary ought to be tough and ready to die and his atheist

---

[48] I.e., French President Marie François Sadi Carnot, 1894; Spanish Prime Minister Cánovas del Castillo, 1897; Elisabeth of Bavaria, Empress of Austria and Queen of Hungary, 1898; King Umberto I of Italy, 1900; US President William McKinley, 1901.

[49] Act to Regulate the Immigration of Aliens into the United States, 1903.

conviction that the idea of God negates reason and human liberty, but uses nothing from Bakunin to back his call for lone man armies.[50]

Similarly, a review of al-Qaida and Islamic State writings that praise the tactics of lone warriors/martyrs/lions as an effective means to strike the enemy points to sources of inspiration other than nineteenth-century anarchism and twentieth-century fascism. One will search in vain for references to Bakunin or Malatesta in the al-Qaida-linked press such as *Inspire* and *al-Malaham* or the Islamic State magazines *Dabiq* and *Rumiyah*. Neither do they refer to white fascist lone wolf advocates James Mason, Louis Beam, David Lane, or Tom Metzger. In fact, these gentlemen are not even mentioned in this literature. The empirical evidence for an anarchist–fascist–al-Qaida and Islamic State connection is simply not there.

The only direct links I have found between the four milieus are between sections of the militant milieus of antiabortionism and white nationalism in the USA. For instance, the website of the Army of God, an organization which caters to a loose network of Christian antiabortion warriors in a "war for the unborn," republished the influential "Leaderless Resistance" essay by white American fascist Louis Beam.[51] *The Army of God Manual*, which provides future warriors with motivation and practical know-how, was in part indebted to white nationalist thought.[52] Individual antiabortion warriors of God have had ties to people and currents in the white nationalist landscape. These have included Michael Griffin, Paul Hill, and Eric Rudolph. Griffin and Hill killed medical doctors David Gunn and John Britton at abortion clinics in Pensacola, Florida, in 1993 and 1994, respectively.[53] Both were inspired by the concept of the white Christian nationalist Phineas Priesthood and by former Ku Klux Klan organizer John Burt, who claimed to be their "spiritual adviser." Rudolph once trained to become a Christian Identity priest in the Church of Israel, Shell County, Missouri. By the time he bombed two abortion clinics (in Atlanta, Georgia and Birmingham, Mississippi), a lesbian bar in Atlanta, and the Olympic Park in Atlanta, Georgia, killing 3 and wounding 150 people, he had left

[50] Mason, 1992a; 1980b; 1985.
[51] Beam, "Leaderless Resistance", Army of God, n.d.
[52] *The Army of God Manual*, n.d. [53] Hill, 2003.

organized white nationalism. "As I became more militant, I decided to keep a safe distance from any organized group," Rudolph explained, except for some personal contacts in the white "Patriot movement."[54]

Insurrectional anarchism, white radical nationalism, Christian antiabortionism, and militant Islamism all developed tactics based on a division of labor between public leaders fanning the flames and unorganized militants responding to their calls but acting without orders or assistance. Despite these similarities, the tactics developed independently of each other in each respective milieu to further quite distinct political aims. All four milieus have a history, but the history is not the same.

3 The History of the Lone Wolf

One day on this meaningless/Journey through life/I met a tall man crying.
I asked him why a strong man wept/He said his race was dying.

Written by David Lane around 1978 and republished in 1994 by 14 Word Press, this poem expressionistically captures the figure of the lone wolf, standing alone, choked with emotions aroused in response to his subjective perception of acute reality. The glorious race to which he belongs is at the brink of extermination, and it all happens on his watch.[55] As the darkness of Mordor expands to engulf the world, the tears of the lone man turn into the glow of burning iron. In the darkest hour, he clenches his fists and checks his gun. The beauty of the white woman, who holds the future of the race in her womb, must not perish. The howl of the lone wolf breaks into the silence of the night, and is picked up by individual brethren howling in distant corners. *We must secure the existence of our people and a future for white children.*

We will return to the drama of the dying race – the notions of racial "genocide," "suicide," "replacement," and "extermination" – in Section 5,

[54] Rudolph, 2013.
[55] The poem was also Breivik's favorite (Breivik, Letter to author, August 5, 2016).

when examining lone wolves' professed motivations. Here, we will trace the tracks of the first wolves across the transforming landscape of white radical nationalism.

"The White Man Has Lost"

"The White Man has lost!", Joseph Tommasi (1951–75) declared in *Strategy for Revolution*. "We are an occupied people in our own land who must now develop a totally different outlook on revolution."[56] In March 1974, Tommasi announced the formation of the National Socialist Liberation Front (NSFL) in El Monte, in the predominantly Hispanic section of East Los Angeles, renowned for youth protest and music, as captured by Frank Zappa in his "Memoirs of El Monte"; the Grateful Dead, Earth, Wind & Fire, The Beatles, and The Beach Boys had all performed there. This was the area to locate the cells of an urban underground, Tommasi reasoned, which would hit in the metropolis and train in the nearby deserts and national forests. Tommasi let go of the uniforms and the open display of political symbols that had been the hallmarks of the American Nazi Party and the Ku Klux Klan(s), as such posturing would only alert law enforcement agencies. The NSLF warrior "has no uniform," Tommasi said. "He could be the bearded long hair sitting next to you on the bus, or the clean-cut store clerk. He could be anyone anywhere."[57] "They dressed like leftwing radicals" of the 1960s and 1970s, white fascist veteran Tom Metzger later recalled. "No armbands, badges or any other identifying trinkets. They grew hair long, and many had beards. They could move through the streets of L.A. without notice."[58]

Already as a teen, Tommasi had joined the National Socialist White People's Party (NSWPP), then led by Mat Koehl, heir of George Lincoln Rockwell's iconic American Nazi Party, which had been the exact opposite: uniforms, swastika armbands, marches, Hitler salutes. The American Nazi Party had put on a public display of what Americans had learned a National Socialist looked like, even to the point of using the term "Nazi," something an historically aware National Socialist would be

[56] Tommasi, 1974a. [57] Tommasi, 1974a.
[58] Metzger, "Joseph Tommasi Tribute," n.d.

reluctant to do.[59] With flying colors, Rockwell had hoped to arouse the masses to defend the privileges of whiteness encoded by American law since the first Immigration and Naturalization Act of 1790 had stipulated that only a "free white person" could be a citizen of the USA. Black people "are not" and "were not" intended to be "included under the word 'Citizens' in the Constitution," said the Supreme Court in 1857, as they constituted a "subordinate and inferior class of being who had been subjugated by the dominant [white] race" and, therefore, "had no rights or privileges."[60]

Now, however, formal white power was challenged everywhere, in each state, city, and county in the USA, and in the overseas colonies in Africa and Asia. White nationalists – Rockwell's stormtroopers, the hooded Ku Klux Klan(s), the suit-and-tie White Citizen Councils, the Minutemen militia – sought to push back. Rockwell used populist rhetoric and publicity stunts to appeal to the white majority: substituting the swastika for the American eagle; protesting the protests; coining "White Power" to riposte the call for Black Power (cf. White Lives Matter); following the Freedom Riders' bus tours of the Deep South in a Hate Bus; demanding rights and freedoms for white people.

None of that had worked. "National Socialist activities have never produced one significant political result in the U.S.A.," Tommasi concluded. The old leaders had failed to seize the opportunity; there had been no arming of the students, no burning of school buses, only "stagnant Prussian tactics" that failed to reach the revolutionary youth. "Winning the hearts and minds of the people takes intense organizing activity and a willingness on the part of the people to get involved and be organized," Tommasi declared. "Both at this time do not exist."[61]

In *Strategy for Revolution*, Tommasi declared the NSLF had "abandoned the mass strategy and adopted the revolutionary concept of the guerilla underground." "Obtaining political power through the electorate" would never work; instead, efforts should focus on "hurting the Enemy through

---

[59] Nazi was once a German slur for "backward farmer," picked up by political opponents to Hitler.

[60] "Transcript of Dred Scott v. Sanford (1857)." [61] Tommasi, 1974b.

force and violence."[62] The NSLF set up autonomous cells ("combat units") of two fighters and a unit leader, operating without a centralized command. In theory, no one knew the numbers, members, locations, and plans of the cells, not even Tommasi; in practice, the units were not that many, and the fighters not always that unknown.[63]

An early proponent of accelerationism, Tommasi stressed the use of violence, "destruction and disorder" as key to "heightening the contradictions" necessary to achieve revolutionary change.[64] "Political terror is the only thing they [the System, the cops, the Blacks, the masses] understand," an NSLF leaflet read. "The future belongs to the few of us still willing to get our hands dirty."[65]

One-Man Armies, Lone Eagles

In August, 1975, Tommasi was shot to death by an NSWPP stormtrooper.[66] James Mason (b. 1952) took charge of the NSLF and its Midwest counterpart, the National Socialist Movement, and relocated the NSLF headquarters to Chillicothe, Ohio. Mason would later develop his own brand of occult fascism, the Universal Order, hailing convicted eco-racial-socialist-cultist Charles Manson the (spiritual) guide of the fascist revolution.[67] As the world was turned on its head with fascism's defeat in 1945, the new leader would be found at the bottom of society, that is, serving life in prison. In the mid-2010s, Mason returned to visibility as the Nestor of accelerationism, with Atomwaffen Division, a stylish network of armed activists with an "autonomous fascist lifestyle," posing in trademark smiling-skull masks.[68]

---

[62] Tommasi, 1974a.

[63] Interview with NSLF veteran Tom Brady (pseudonym), August 19, 1998.

[64] Tommasi, 1974b; 1974a. [65] NSLF, 1974.

[66] Tommasi had donated his family house to the NSWPP to use as its Los Angeles headquarters. After the fallout with Koehl, Tommasi lost his inheritance. In a subsequent skirmish outside the house on August 15, 1975, Tommasi was killed by stormtroopers.

[67] Mason, 1986. [68] *Atomwaffen Division*, n.d.

Echoing Tommasi, Mason was convinced that the national socialist effort to rally the "white masses" "won't work, never has worked, and almost always results in merely revealing our weaknesses and making us look like idiots."[69] In his monthly magazine *Siege* (1980–1986), Mason called for immediate action to "smash the system." The revolution would depend on deeds, not words, and would not wait for the white masses to awaken.[70]

Instead, Mason suggested the white masses should be treated as cowards.

> They say a coward will allow himself to be bullied and backed up as long as there is room left for him to back up. All of White America has been behaving like a damned coward in the face of arrogant Blacks and traitors in government dismantling the once-great United States of America. Before it is too late, let's see to it that the big coward at last gets backed into a corner so that he is going to have to come out fighting![71]

It only takes a few white assassins who, independently of one another, randomly kill Black people in a handful of cities to incite Black folks to seek revenge on white people, Mason reasoned. "If we can't get the Whites off their asses to retake control of their destiny then we can at least put them in a position where they will have to fight for their miserable lives!"[72]

Mason radicalized Tommasi's autonomous cell tactics by suggesting the "concept of the One-Man Army" to "bring the struggle to the Enemy"; "Wherever you may be at this moment, let the revolution be there also." Letting the Jews, the Blacks, the bureaucrats, the police pigs "die the death they so richly deserve" is "well within the capacities of a small band of fanatics, each member a one-man army."[73] When you join the armed underground, Mason wrote, "two participants are one too many."[74]

---

[69] Mason, 1981d. [70] Mason, 1981b. [71] Mason, 1980a. [72] Mason, 1980a.
[73] Mason, 1981c. [74] Mason, 1981d.

In *Terrorism*, issued as a special supplement to *Siege*, Mason hailed four white racist assassins as exemplary "Lone Eagles": Fredrick Cowan,[75] Frank Spisak,[76] Joseph Gerard Christopher, and Joseph Paul Franklin.[77] Mason named Christopher, an army private who killed random black people on the streets of New York City, Richmond, and Buffalo, "The Great White Hope." "From Buffalo we now have reports of Blacks stoning and shooting at Whites," Mason exclaimed. Do the "mathematics of terror." Fan the flames. Bring on the apocalypse.[78]

Mason saved most praise for Joseph Paul Franklin, the white racist serial killer who left the NSWPP and the Ku Klux Klan to embark on a "holy war against evildoers: interracial couples, blacks, and Jews" as "executioner, the judge, and the jury."[79] To Mason, Franklin was a "gift from God," "an American revolutionary hero" who did everything right.[80] He did not belong to an organization, did not openly talk politics, used faked IDs, and operated strictly on his own. "We tell you flatly to NEVER engage in conspiracy," Mason emphasized. Franklin "didn't and look at what's been accomplished! No conspiracy there, just the strike of lightning," "like our ancient gods of thunder."[81]

"Franklin was only one man," Mason exclaimed. "What if a dozen or more had followed his example?" To Mason, people like Franklin did more for the white revolution than white nationalist organizations. "They *are* the Movement, because only they are moving."[82] Unsurprisingly, such opinions did not sit well among white nationalist organizations. Mason's radicalism gained a boost in the 1990s when the issues and supplements of *Siege*

---

[75] Cowan killed four black and one Indian co-worker at his former workplace in New Rochelle, New York, on Valentine's Day, 1977, before committing suicide-by-cop. To Mason, Cowan was a "one-man Einsatzgruppe" (NSM Michigan, *A Brief History of American National Socialism*, n.d.; Mason, 1992b).

[76] Former NSWWP member Frank Spisak shot and killed two black men and a man he mistook for a Jew at Cleveland State University in 1982 (Spisak, letter in Mason, 1992c).

[77] Warthan, "Terrorism," n.d.   [78] Mason, 1992d.

[79] Franklin, cited in Ayton, 2011, p. 2.   [80] Mason, 1981a.   [81] Mason, 1992e.

[82] Mason, 1992e.

were published in an edited volume by radical traditionalist Michael Moynihan, and yet again twenty years later when #ReadSiege and lone wolf attacks trended in the postdigital fascist culture of the 2010s.

Leaderless Resistance

The first more profound outline of lone wolf tactics to reach a wider public was Louis Beam's essay "Leaderless Resistance," which would give the tactics its name. Originally published in 1983 in *The Inter-Klan Newsletter & Survival Alert*,[83] it made its breakthrough when republished in *The Seditionist* in 1992.

In 1992, the Soviet Union was gone, and George H. W. Bush fed the conspiracy-exposing industry by referring to the "New World Order." Then came Clinton and the federal assaults on the Weaver family in Ruby Ridge (1992) and the Students of the Seventh Seal (Branch Davidian) compound in Waco (1993) – two events used to illustrate federal monstrosity. Clinton's gun control legislation – the 1993 Brady bill[84] and the 1994 Federal Assault Weapons Ban[85] – was interpreted as an initial step to deprive Americans of the right to bear arms. It was as if William Pierce's *Turner Diaries*, written under the pseudonym Andrew Macdonald, was coming true.

In William Pierce's bestselling race war novel, the US government bans the private possession of firearms and stages "Gun Raids" in which black government agents invade the homes of decent white Americans in search of their guns, bringing offenders to mass detention centers. In *Turner Diaries*, the great majority of white Americans, patriot militias included, give up their guns and thereby their freedoms. Were it not for the "Order," a handful of dedicated dissidents (branded "fascists" by the government)

---

[83] Beam, 1983.

[84] The Brady Handgun Violence Prevention Act mandated a federal background check and a five-day waiting period for firearm purchase.

[85] The Public Safety and Recreational Firearms Use Protection Act prohibited the manufacture, transfer, or possession of semiautomatic assault weapons for civilian use for a ten-year period.

who saw what was coming and planned ahead, the white revolution that the novel portrays would not have been possible.[86]

By 1992, two events provided Beam with an audience for his critique of organized resistance. The early 1980s had seen the rise and fall of the Brüders Schweigen, an Aryan guerilla group in Washington/Idaho nicknamed the Order after *Turner Diaries*. Led by Odinist Robert J. Mathews (1953–1984), the brotherhood was conceived as a "Holy Order" of initiates organized to "deliver our people from the Jew and bring total victory to the Aryan race."[87] The oathbound brethren raised a multimillion-dollar war chest through armed car robberies and counterfeit operations, allowing for huge donations to white nationalist projects and the acquisition of military equipment, arms, cars, motorcycles, safe houses, and land, on which the Order built an Aryan Academy training camp. When the Order launched a bombing and assassination campaign, the FBI mobilized informants to track down its leadership, including Bob Mathews, who was killed in a 1984 shoot-out. Had they not built an organization, radicals retrospectively reflected, the FBI would have nowhere from which to recruit collaborators.[88]

There followed the 1988 Fort Smith sedition trial, in which fourteen white nationalist leaders were accused of conspiring to overthrow the government and establish an all-white nation in the Pacific Northwest. The defendants included six members of the Order, five members of the Covenant, the Sword, the Arm of the Lord, and three ideologues: Richard G. Butler of the Aryan Nations, Robert E. Miles, Imperial Kludd (national chaplain) of the United Klans of America, and Louis Beam, Texas Grand Dragon Emeritus of the Knights of the Ku Klux Klan. Acting as government-protected witnesses were several members of white nationalist organizations, including Glenn Miller of the Carolina Knights of the Ku Klux Klan and the White Patriot Party, and James D. Ellison, head of the Covenant, the Sword, the Arm of the Lord. The defendants were acquitted,

---

[86] Macdonald [Pierce], 1980 [1978]. [87] Flynn & Gerhardt, 1999; Gardell, 2003.

[88] Duey, Interview, May 20, 1997; Hawthorne, Interview, October 2, 1996; Lane, Interview, November 12, 1996; Kemp, Interview, May 8, 1997; Yabrough, Interview, April 15, 1997; Tate, Interview, May 22, 1997.

but the experience constituted another blow to the idea of organized resistance. Asked how the trial affected the white movement, defendant Robert E. Miles replied, "What movement? What's left of it after this?"[89]

In *Leaderless Resistance*, Beam urges white nationalists to rethink their mode of organizing. Based on his experience, Beam concludes that the pyramid model is "not only useless, but extremely dangerous for the participants when in it is utilized in a resistance movement." Obviously, "organizations utilizing this method of command and control are easy prey for government infiltration, entrapment and destruction."[90] Beam warns against the call for "white unity." "From the point of view of tyrants and ... police agencies, nothing is more desirable than that those who oppose them be UNIFIED in their command structure, and that every person who opposes them belong to a pyramid type group. Such groups and organizations are an easy kill."[91]

Instead, Beam suggests the concept of leaderless resistance, a system of organized non-organization based on "very small or even one-man cells of resistance" operating without "any central control or direction." Cells and individuals should "operate independently" and "never report to a central headquarters or a single leader" for instruction. "The last thing federal snoops would have, if they had any choice in the matter, is a thousand different small phantom cells opposing them," Beam argues. "Such a situation is an intelligence nightmare for a government intent upon knowing everything they possibly can about those who oppose them."[92]

The Phineas Priesthood

In the early 1990s, lone wolf tactics was embraced within Christian Identity as Phineas acts of divine justice.

A heterogeneous family of congregations and Bible study groups, Christian Identity claims that whites are the Chosen People, the real Israel. Semitic Jews are impostors who seek to deprive Aryans of their birthright. Convinced that the Hebrew Bible really is about them, Identity believers typically observe the Sabbath, celebrate Passover and Purim,

---

[89] Cited in Simmons, 1988; cf. Stern, 2000;The Covenant, 1982; Barkun, 1995; Kaplan, 1997a.

[90] Beam, 1992. [91] Beam, 1992. [92] Beam, 1992.

follow the dietary rules of Leviticus and Deuteronomy, take Hebrew names, and use the ancient Israeli YHWH or Yahweh, Yah or I-Am for God and Yahshua or Yahweh-Yahshua for Jesus.[93]

According to Identity, only whites are fully human and descendants of Adam and Eve; only whites are living souls, that is, embodiments of God. "Ye are gods," said the Lord (Psa. 82:6) to His Chosen, "children of the most High." African and Native Americans are pre-Adamic "livestock" and "wild animals" (Gen. 1:24), created to serve the Adamic race. Jews are of the post-Adamic "serpent race," the seed of Cain, spawn of the Devil.

As embodiments of good and evil, whites and Jews are locked in an apocalyptic war of world dominion. Identity rejects the Rapture scenario, popular among American evangelicals, in which God moves believers to a heavenly refuge before the Apocalypse. In Identity teaching, there is no escape. "God will use His people to establish His kingdom on earth," explained John Baumgardner of the Black Knights of the Ku Klux Klan. "It's gonna be a total war, a revolutionary war, and as Israel we'll have to fight!"[94]

To Baumgardner, America is the Holy Land. "God said to Israel: 'Go in and kill every human being and then possess the land'."[95] In Numbers 33:55, God warns His people, "But if you do not drive out the inhabitants of the land, those you allow to remain will become barbs in your eyes and thorns in your sides." This, Baumgardner emphasizes, is what plagues white America to this day. As Israel (white Americans) let Indigenous people survive in reservations, imported black slaves, and allowed nonwhite immigration, they aroused the wrath of God. "We, who are part of Israel, are punished today for that very reason," Baumgardner exclaimed. Thus, the need for the Phineas Priesthood.[96]

The Phineas concept is derived from Numbers 25:1–13. Men of Israel "indulged in sexual immorality" with Moabite women, "and the LORD's anger burned." He orders Moses to chop off the heads of the offenders and

[93] Gardell, 2003; 2004; McFarland & Gottfried, 2002.

[94] Baumgardner, Interview, November 1, 1996.

[95] Baumgardner, Interview, November 1, 1996.

[96] Baumgardner, Interview, November 1, 1996.

sends a plague, killing 24,000 Israelis. In the midst of this calamity, Phineas, grandson of Aaron, sees an Israeli man bring a Moabite woman into his tent. Phineas pursues them and drives his spear through the couple, killing them both in the act. Pleased, God declares that Phineas has turned His "wrath away from the children of Israel." God institutes a "covenant of an everlasting priesthood" with Phineas as the guardian of divine law on earth. Since then, Identity theologians Robert Alan Balaicius and Richard Kelly Hoskins claim, an underground priesthood of righteous zealots have operated as God's executioners. "The Phinehas Priest is God's commando," Balaicius asserts. He works "alone, without the collusion of others," zealously putting "miscegenators (blood-mixers) and idolaters to death."[97]

Richard Kelly Hoskins' *Vigilantes of Christendom: The History of the Phineas Priesthood* (1990) was the first, and arguably the most influential, major work celebrating the "everlasting Western priesthood."[98] For years, Hoskins corresponded with white nationalists incarcerated for killing "mixed-race" couples, homosexuals, abortion doctors, blacks, and Jews, or for refusing to pay taxes to "the Synagogue of Satan," the federal government. "They believe that their god has called them to do their dangerous work," Hoskins concludes.[99]

Hoskins details the legend of an unbroken lineage of righteous avengers, from St George, King Arthur, Robin Hood, and Jesse James to scores of individual vigilantes forgotten by history as they worked clandestinely and never sought credit for their heroic deeds. Hoskins praises the Phineas priests for, as he claims, having executed Abraham Lincoln and John F. Kennedy, and tax-resister Gordon Kahl, who killed two US marshals and was shot to death after a manhunt.[100]

When Israel strays from God's Law, Hoskins writes, God sends calamities, such as the Haitian Revolution and the Southern Reconstruction, which to Hoskins serve as warnings of what the future will entail if God's Law is not reinstated. During Reconstruction, "the symbol '#25' (signifying Numbers 25) appeared on walls and sidewalks" as Phineas priests

---

[97] Balaicius, 1997, pp. 139, 142.
[98] Hoskins, 1990.
[99] Hoskins, 1990, p. viii. [100] Hoskins, 1990, pp. 201–212; Corcoran, 1990.

initiated a nationwide hunt for blacks who were out of place. "It was as if fresh air blew through the land," Hoskins writes, and by "extralegal executions" (lynchings), white rule was reinstalled.[101] History is now repeating itself, Hoskins states. Establishment tyranny will give birth to the "age of Phineas." Transgressors be warned: "It makes little difference whether you agree or disagree with the Phineas Priesthood. It is important that you know that it exists, is active, and in the near future may become a central fact in your life."[102]

The Holy 14 Words

A milestone in the evolution of white nationalist lone wolf tactics was coining of the "14 Words" by David Lane (1938–2007): "We must secure the existence of our people and a future for white children." Through the 14 Words, white unity of organization can be substituted for unity of purpose, which fits the tactics of leaderless resistance envisioned by Beam. According to Lane, "The highest law of nature is the preservation of one's kind." "The 14 words are holy. They are decreed by the Gods. They give you a divine mission. Live them, and fight smart."[103]

A former Klan organizer and Aryan Nations member-turned-Odinist, Lane was a founding member of the Order, but was not present with Mathews in the 1984 shoot-out. He was eventually apprehended in 1985 and sentenced to 190 years. Lane was also charged, but acquitted, in the 1988 Fort Smith sedition trial. Lane claims that the 14 Words were revealed to him during the manhunt, when he ventured out in the Chihuahuan desert in New Mexico to meditate for "forty days and forty nights" to find a way to save the white race from dying. He called out to the "Watchers," a group of Aryan sages whom he identifies with Blavatsky's Guides of the Aryan race. Lane says that the Watchers commissioned him to summon the Aryan elite of the white race, and revealed the holy 14 Words to him for this purpose, only days before his arrest.[104]

Looking at the white nationalist organizations of his time, Lane found them misguided politically and organizationally – more freaks than

---

[101] Hoskins, 1990, pp. 22, 330–333. [102] Hoskins, 1990, pp. 420, vii.

[103] Lane, Interview, November 12, 1996. [104] Lane, Interview, November 12, 1996.

a serious challenge to the system – and dismissed the "One-hundred percent Americanism" of the Ku Klux Klan and the gun-toting, flag-waving militias as CRAP (Christian Rightwing American Patriots). To Lane, the United States government was an enemy of the white race, as evidenced by its assault on the Southern Confederacy, its war against National Socialist Germany, and its betrayal of white Rhodesia and white South Africa. While acknowledging that "many rank-and-file patriots" are "good-hearted people," Lane stresses that white radicals flying the Star-Spangled Banner are "beyond irrational." "What flag flies in the courtrooms of the Federal judges who order the mixing and extermination of our race?" he asks rhetorically. Stressing the difference between the "white wing" and the "right wing," Lane claims that one cannot be loyal to both the white race and to America. "How can you *be* what destroys you?"[105]

According to Lane, white Americans should realize that they "live in an occupied country" (the Zionist Occupation Government), and can no longer afford to trust the institutions, the police, and the military. How do you navigate in enemy territory? How do you wage an armed resistance under an occupation without external backing from another country? Surveillance technology allows the modern state to control its territory in minute detail, and no national liberation army base would go undetected for any sustained period of time, not even in areas of vast wilderness. Lane's experience with the Order made him realize that the classic guerilla tactics of small mobile units would not work either, as they would be far too organized and therefore easy to scout, infiltrate, monitor, and round up. Its time might come, but a later stage in the struggle to establish a white racial state. The only viable alternative is to build a "strictly separated revolutionary structure" with a division of labor between an overt milieu of propaganda outlets and a covert milieu of armed militants. Since the public leaders "will be under scrutiny," they need to "operate within the [legal] parameters" and the windshield of the Bill of Rights, using the instruments of democracy to dismantle democracy. Leaders need to stay "rigidly separated" from militants and any criminal activity. Individuals entering the leaderless underground of armed resistance (Will of the Aryan Nations,

---

[105] Lane, 1994a; 1996; 1994b, pp. 7, 9.

WOTAN, in Lane's parlance) should be ready to sacrifice their lives to secure the survival of their kind. The WOTAN paramilitary "must operate in small, autonomous cells, the smaller the better, even one man alone."[106] Armed activists should "live like chameleons" – melt into the mainstream community and "change hats" when prudent to avoid suspicion.[107]

The one aim of violent activity is to "hasten the demise of the system before it totally destroys our gene pool" by utilizing "fire, bombs, guns, terror, disruption and destruction. Weak points in the infrastructure of an industrialized society are primary targets. Whatever and whoever perform valuable services for the system are targets, human or otherwise. Special attention and merciless terror are visited upon those White men who commit race treason."[108]

I met with Lane during the aftermath of the 1995 bombing of a federal office complex in Oklahoma City. Of the 168 lives claimed, 19 were small children, as the buildings housed a daycare center for the children of federal employees. Asking Lane if it was not counterproductive to kill innocent babies, many of them white, he shook his head. "[T]here are no innocents when your people face extinction. ... There is no middle ground. Only those that are for your cause and those who are your enemies."[109] To Lane, the Oklahoma City bombing was exemplary. No one saw it coming. There was no organization to infiltrate, no communication to tap, no leader to snare – only dedicated action. Resistance should be wherever the enemy is: everywhere.

The Law of the Wolf

Much like David Lane, White Aryan Resistance (WAR, est. 1983) founder Tom Metzger (1938–2020) stressed the distinction between the "right wing" and "the white wing." Metzger was a former member of the John Birch

---

[106] Lane, 1994a, p. 14.   [107] Lane, Interview, November 12, 1996.

[108] Lane, 1994a. When the text was reissued in *Deceived, Damned and Defiant: The Revolutionary Writings of David Lane*, (1997, p. 47) the list of targets was substituted with the phrase "of course, in occupied countries, the overt arm of the revolution must not detail specifics."

[109] Lane, Interview, November 12, 1996.

Society, the Posse Comitatus, The New Christian Crusade Church, the Minutemen, the Knights of the Ku Klux Klan (David Duke's Klan), the California Knights of the Ku Klux Klan (his own Klan), the Klan Border Watch, and the White American Political Association. Having once won the Democratic Party's primary in the 43rd Congressional District of California (southern Los Angeles, 1980) and going on to organize fascist black-shirt squads with helmets, shields, and sticks in an effort to dominate the streets of a white working-class area of Los Angeles, Metzger said he had had his share of organized white nationalism.[110] The same goes for organized religion. He preached the gospel of the Ku Klux Klan, converted to Catholicism, was an ordained Identity minister, camped with Odinism, and passed by the Church of the Creator into a secular outlook. "Our race is our religion," Metzger emphasized. "WAR will not allow religious theories and unproven myths to interfere with Aryan survival and advancement."[111]

A "third position" fascist who stressed white working-class rights and racial socialism, Metzger pioneered the cut-the-crap straight-talk gutter-style racism picked up by Andrew Anglin's *Daily Stormer* and the fascist YouTubers of the 2020s. Metzger's outreach efforts included a TV show, *Race and Reason* (on cable since 1983); *WAR* magazine, boosted as "the most racist newspaper on earth"; a WAR Fax distribution net; the "WAR Hotline" talk-radio show; and various homepages and social media platforms, some established already at the dawn of the Internet revolution. WAR formally went bankrupt after a 1990 Southern Poverty Law Center civil suit that argued that two Portland skinheads who murdered black student Mulugeta Seraw were acting under the influence of WAR propaganda, but Metzger remained an active proponent of leaderless resistance tactics.[112]

Organized white nationalism will remain a small minority, fighting the small minority in power, Metzger argued. Per definition, the white masses constitute a herd in which each animal is concerned with her own security

---

[110] Metzger, Interview, December 16, 1996.

[111] Metzger, "White Aryan Resistance Positions," n.d.

[112] Metzger, Interview, December 16, 1996; Metzger, "Mini Manual for Survival," n.d.; Michael, 2016.

and material needs, which makes her conform with the crowd. The quest for honor and heroism is the domain of the dedicated few who will secure racial survival. As the white revolution "can't move much further with the right wing in our way," Metzger stresses accelerationism; systemic collapse will come from the contradictions inherent to the system itself. The root of the problem is global capitalism; the "racial problems are a side issue that comes from economic problems caused by the multinational corporations." "As the rich are getting richer and the poor are getting poorer and the massive influx of people from other nations, mostly nonwhite ... you know, the chemistry is there, it's like a bomb, waiting for someone to light the fuse." Metzger points at violent protests in the depressed black and Hispanic communities as moments of breakdown to capitalize on. What white revolutionaries should do now is increase the tensions, fanning the flames by "advocating [white racist] violence; promoting violence; inspiring violence."[113]

To this end, Metzger encourages lone wolf operations. Let go of membership organizations, forget dues, uniforms, and meetings, Metzger advised in the "Mini Manual for Survival." Do not announce who you are. "Wearing racial symbols is not wise and creates a possible no-win situation." Resistance should be based on small autonomous cells, preferably one-man units. "Three people can keep a secret if two are dead!" Acquire appropriate skills by studying online manuals. Military weapons are not necessary. "There are plenty of weapons lying around": rocks, bottles, bricks, wrenches, hammers; even cars or a ballpoint pen can be turned into a weapon if used properly. After a strike, "go where least expected. Large urban areas are much easier to disappear in than open country or woods." Remember, Metzger adds, do not let them kid you: "the end does justify the means!"[114]

"Anyone is capable of being a Lone Wolf," Metzger wrote in "Laws of the Lone Wolf," summarizing the basics. Never join a membership group. Stay away from meetings, rallies, conventions, concerts, and rendezvous. Start off small. Many small victories are better than one big blunder. Learn

[113] Metzger, Interview, December 16, 1996; December 15, 1998.

[114] Metzger, "Mini Manual for Survival," n.d.

from your mistakes and the mistakes of others. Never rush. Plan carefully. The less any outsider knows, the safer and more successful you will be. Never keep records. Repeated activity in one place will lead to increased attention there. The more you adjust tactics, the more effective you become. Random chaos is non-predictable. Others will notice your activities, but never try to take credit. Success should be all the recognition you need. "Exist and fight as lone wolves and you will last longer and be at peak performance. Remember, those who have come before you are counting on you, those who will come after you are depending on you. Think White, act White, be White!"[115] Simple rules; hard to follow.

4 Wolves of the North

In the 1990s, lone wolf leaderless resistance tactics began to spread across what white nationalists call "the once-white world." It coincided with the formation of a globalized white power culture, animated by a new generation of activists brought in during the late 1980s and 1990s through music, fashion, and digital culture, which (literally) infused new life into a milieu that had begun to look like a retirement home for old people. The white power culture arose from the merger of European fascism and American white supremacy, two racial orders in which whites had held but lost constitutional power. Being dethroned left white nationalists humiliated, confused, and revanchist, and enabled them to claim the position of the underdog. Too young to remember "the good old days" in the 1930s Europe and 1950s America they felt nostalgic for, the new generation of fascists saw themselves as a "resistance." Cultivating a sense of betrayal, they vowed to "regain" the power, resources, and privileges "they" (as members of their race) had once had and still felt entitled to.

In 1994, the apartheid regime of South Africa fell. Around 1 million white people, one fifth of its white population, left for another country in the British Commonwealth, including Australia, New Zealand, Canada, and the USA. Dislocated white South Africans added to the white power culture by

---

[115] Metzger, 2010.

providing horror stories of life under black tyranny and fueled the desire to reestablish a white ethnostate somewhere, anywhere, everywhere.

The white power culture was anti-egalitarian and essentialist in its understanding of race, culture, ethnicity, and gender. Beyond bringing together American white supremacy and European fascism – symbolized by the fiery swastika – the white power culture was open to other causes lost or ridiculed, ranging from pagan traditions, conspiracy theories, sunken continents, and space Aryans to biodynamic farming.[116] In previous studies, I discussed the bewildering array of "stuff" found in the white nationalist landscape through the metaphor of "the smorgasbord of the white power counterculture."[117] Of course, the diverse treats were not appreciated by everyone, and there have been a series of efforts to unite the race, clear the table, and substitute the smorgasbord with a set menu. Despite the stress on hierarchy, discipline, order, and the leader principle, no such effort has so far succeeded. On the contrary, new dishes are constantly offered based on the latest conspiracy theory, fascist fad, or obsession.

By 2021, the white power culture was seen as too subcultural for mainstream white nationalist taste, but the smorgasbord is still there. White nationalists from different walks of life gather around the table, including lone wolves in the making, such as the Last Rhodesian, the Pittsburgh Synagogue Shooter, and the Templar Knight. The atrocities of these particular individuals have drawn the world's attention to the white nationalist cause and contribute to the stories told around the table.

Individual lone wolves put together their own particular plates by picking from the various dishes offered, as illustrated by the 1,500-page cut-and-paste compilation *2083: A Declaration of European Independence* that Anders Behring Breivik offered as an explanation for his 2011 massacre. Composed around a wide array of themes Breivik had encountered at the table and wanted to tell the world about, *2083* includes Islamophobia, conservative nationalism, radical traditionalism, fascism, anti-feminism, (white) indigenous rights, cultural and biological racism, right-wing evangelical theology, the Knights Templar tradition, warrior ideals, lone wolf tactics, and blueprints of the white revolution. Many parts of the *2083*

---

[116] Barkun, 1998; 2006. [117] Gardell, 1998b; 2003.

compilation do not fit well together, reflecting the internal contradictions within the landscape of white nationalism. Breivik rails against national socialism, yet includes national socialist texts; he takes exception to racism, yet excels in racist propositions; he barks at anti-Semitism, yet retains an anti-Semitic agenda.[118]

The rise of the white power culture came at the end of the Cold War. The communist threat was gone. The West was the winner of the day. Mainstream American intellectuals proclaimed Pax Americana, the end of history, and the last man. A market economy, liberal democracy, and neoliberal policies with privatization, the outsourcing of public functions, and new public management expanded across the world to reach a hegemonic status as "the natural order of things," to which there was no viable alternative.

The globalization of neoliberal market economy aroused fears that it would spur gross inequalities, environmental destruction, and level all other cultures and ways of doing things. Resistance was everywhere, as evidenced by the multitude of global social justice movements.[119] However, globalization also reinforced white nationalist narratives of racial genocide and antiwhite global conspiracies and invited white resistance to be articulated in terms of a legitimate fight for (white) "indigenous rights."

Importantly, the end of the Cold War marked the point at which the processes of globalization entered their current – and far from completed – phase, characterized by the fact that there is no society outside of global society. The emergence of a global society carries with it the elimination of an outside; there is no other world beyond this one. If there is no outside, the solution must be inherent to the system; radical change has to come from within. Within the political landscape of white nationalism, this strengthened the revolutionary theory of accelerationism. The system will collapse by increasing its internal contradictions. A means to hasten the coming of Ragnarök is violent terror – the more irrational, the better. Hence, the path lies open for the lone wolf.

[118] Gardell, 2014; Breivik, 2011; Breivik, Letter to author, February 21, 2014.
[119] Hardt & Negri, 2001; 2005.

Two Types of Wolf: The Franklin Model versus the McVeigh Model

When lone wolf leaderless resistance tactics spread among white nationalists across the global North, it had evolved into two basic models or schools of tactics: the Franklin model and the McVeigh model, named after Joseph Paul Franklin and Timothy McVeigh, respectively.

Franklin was the white racist serial killer hailed as exemplary by James Mason in *Siege* and to whom William Pierce in 1989 dedicated his race war novel *Hunter*: "the Lone Hunter, who saw his duty as a White man and did what a responsible son of his race must do."[120] Between 1977 and 1980, Franklin crisscrossed the USA, assassinating an estimated twenty-two individuals: Jews, young black people, race-mixed couples, and white women who had "defiled their race" by dating black men. He operated strictly under the radar. He was unorganized, did not communicate with other white nationalists, did not participate in white power marches or events, and evaded the police by changing states, cities, guns, and modus operandi of the murders. At times he appeared disguised as a nonwhite man, biked between his temporal sniper nest and his getaway car, and only slayed people whom he had no prior relations with, in areas where he was unknown. "That was all part of a plan to start a race war," Franklin said, by creating "enough tensions that eventually blacks and whites ... would be going at it."[121]

McVeigh committed the Oklahoma City bombings of April 19, 1995. While certain scholars of lone wolf terrorism would exclude him from their datasets as he (most likely) had an accomplice, Terry Nichols, his deed is generally hailed as an exemplary lone wolf operation within the landscape of white radical nationalism. He was unorganized and operated below the radar of the police; as a result, no one saw the act coming. He shocked the nation and drew attention to his cause. While he did not write a manifesto, he motivated his attack in two statements, "An Essay of Hypocrisy" and a "Letter of Explanation" to Fox News, the latter text including a section in which the perpetrator interviews himself, an essayistic device adopted by subsequent lone wolves in their manifestos.

[120] Macdonald [Pierce], 1989. [121] Ayton, 2011.

McVeigh frequented gun shows as a vendor, where he came across white power publications. He contemplated "a campaign of individual assassination," but opted for a bombing of the kind described in *Turner Diaries*. That would be an exemplary "retaliatory strike; a counter attack" that would "take the fight to the enemy" by preemptively destroying an enemy command and control center.[122]

McVeigh declared that he only did what the USA had been doing in Iraq and Serbia. Whether a bomb was delivered by truck or plane mattered little to its victims. In Iraq, too, there were daycare centers in the government buildings bombed by American planes, and the US bombings also killed civilians, then referred to as collateral damage. To McVeigh, the Oklahoma City bombing was a message, to show the people what was going on. "Many foreign nations and peoples hate Americans for the very reasons most Americans loathe me. Think about that."[123]

The Franklin and McVeigh models represent two different tactics. The Franklin model is a low-intensity campaign of terror. It uses serial assassinations to send a message to the targeted communities of racialized others (blacks, Muslims, Roma, Jews) or designated internal enemies (race traitors, feminists, cultural Marxists) that the victims are forced to represent by being killed: you are out of place, unwanted, worthless, have got to go. The McVeigh model represents a high-intensity strike of terror – an unexpected attack so shocking that the nation halts, all eyes on the crime. Both models count on the media to play their role; the first model predicts that the media will initially blame the victims/the targeted community and then slowly build the terror with stories of the serial killer on the loose; the second trusts that the media will amplify the deed by broadcasting everything about it, including its carnage, motif, and perpetrator.

From the perpetrator's perspective, the Franklin model is less risky. By operating under the radar, changing the modus operandi, and killing people whom the perpetrator has no prior relation with, in places where he or she is not known, the perpetrator seeks to avoid getting caught. Lone wolves following the Franklin model may never be identified, and some wait years

---

[122] McVeigh, 2001. [123] McVeigh, 1998; 2001.

Schools of the Lone Wolf

Franklin Model	McVeigh Model
Low-intensity	High-intensity
Serial killings	Massacre, bombing
Low risk of getting caught	High risk of getting caught, death
Low immediate impact, terror increases with time	High immediate impact, terror decreases with time
Rare publication of manifesto, public statement	Publication of manifesto, public statement
Use of court to communicate tactics to selected recipients	Use of court to broadcast political views
Desire for followers	Desire for followers
Seeking of heroic status, immortality	Seeking of heroic status, immortality

after their first killings before starting a new cycle, perhaps in another area or state. The McVeigh model puts the perpetrator at high risk of being caught or killed during or shortly after wreaking chaos through a big assault. The McVeigh model is a high-risk, high-gain venture; the media attention, impact, and political upheaval are much greater. The chances of having the political message disseminated nationwide or even worldwide are considerably higher. Few Franklin-style serial terrorists risk revealing themselves by publishing a manifesto or issuing a public declaration. To lone wolves following the McVeigh model, publishing a manifesto or delivering a declaration is close to mandatory. In addition, should the perpetrator survive, the trial can be used as a platform to announce his or her political grievances and ideology.

The Race Warrior versus the Templar Knight

Among white nationalists, the two models are recurrently compared, evaluated, and debated. Let me exemplify with the debate over the approaches of Peter Mangs, the Swedish serial killer who followed the

Franklin model, and Anders Behring Breivik, who followed the McVeigh model. As Mangs is less known to an international audience than Breivik, I will present Mangs' deeds, tactics, and motivations in detail, in a way not necessary with Breivik. In Mangs' case, the brief is based on ten interviews, each of three hours, that I conducted with him in prison, as well as his own writings and my fieldwork in Malmö, where I talked to relatives of his victims, survivors, people in the targeted community, and scores of white nationalists that hailed his deeds as heroic. The Breivik brief is based on my four-hour interview with him after his sentencing, our correspondence over the years, his own writings, and talks with scores of supporters. In both cases, the police investigations and trial proceedings also provided material.[124]

Peter Mangs is the most effective and politically conscious lone wolf known in Sweden. Operating in Malmö between 2003 and 2010, Mangs launched what he named a "terror war against multiculturalism" by killing three and trying to kill at least twelve more people he identified as Muslim, black, or Roma by their appearance or their name. One of his victims was a young white Swedish woman he killed for being with a man he took for Muslim. Well versed in race war literature (including *Turner Diaries* and *Hunter*), Mangs sought to "ignite the starting motor of a full-scale race war" by amplifying tensions between various classes of people in the increasingly segregated city.[125]

Peter Mangs was thirty-one years old when he killed his first randomly selected victim in 2003. He did not smoke or drink and kept in shape by bicycling and taekwondo, earning a black belt at the dojang where he served as webmaster and treasurer. A musician by training, who played bass guitar (funk, jazz, dixie), Mangs studied nursing but worked as a dental technician until 2009, six years into his racist killing campaign, when he signed off to become a full-time race warrior. At six feet tall and slender with blue eyes, short hair, and proper manners, Mangs passed as the ordinary Joe on the streets of Malmö or at the City Library, where he studied national socialism, lone wolf tactics, Odinism, Ariosophy, anti-Semitism, and conspiracy literature. He composed a manifesto, the *German Philosophy*, built on the

---

[124] Gardell, 2015a; 2018; 2017; 2014.

[125] Mangs, Interview, June, 16, 2014; cf. Gardell, 2015a.

model of Nietzsche's *The Gay Science*, including short poems and aphorisms, each with a headline and arranged alphabetically. It was not for publication but was intended as his testimony to the Aryan elite, the New Man that would be galvanized through the apocalyptic race war he sought to achieve. The *German Philosophy*, Mangs claims, sprung from the depths of the Aryan racial soul. "I don't study much, I listen inwards for the whispers of the *Deutsche Volk-Seele*." Identifying fascism as the resurfacing of psychic forces embedded in the Aryan collective unconscious, Mangs sought to unfetter the force of Wotan to save the race at the brink of its doom. History is a war between the races. Were Aryans and Jews to meet in open battle, white victory would be certain. However, Jews play by list and proxies. They have opened every Western country except Israel for non-white migration. The black and Muslim "invaders" come "armed with non-Aryan genes. They need no guns," Mangs states. "Cultural integration and holocaust are the same thing for blond people. Death is death, either way." Indoctrinated in the false doctrines of equality, social justice, nonviolence, human rights, and Christian ethics, the white masses abstain from fighting for their own survival. Responsibility falls hard on the shoulders of the Aryan elite. Mangs sees himself as a self-realized Nietzschean superman whose nature was key to racial survival. "Kindness," Mangs says, "will be the death of the Aryan race," whereas "extreme brutality" is imperative. "I don't have the same limitations and inhibitions that the surrounding individuals have therefore I could be the one that defines the future of our identity."[126]

Having studied the modus operandi of Joseph Paul Franklin, Mangs applied the Franklin model to the city of Malmö. He only shot people with whom he had no prior relation, choosing his victims by their names or looks, changing city quarters, guns, and modus operandi according to irregular patterns, using a bicycle as a getaway vehicle, and cruising the city at night disguised as an "immigrant" with a dark tan and brown contact lenses. "The plan was to expand the operation throughout Sweden," Mangs said. "Hit at various locations, distract the police investigation."[127]

---

[126] Mangs, *German Philosophy*, n.d. For Mangs' writings, see Gardell, 2015a; 2018b.
[127] Mangs, Interview, November 10, 2013; June 16, 2014.

Mangs aimed his guns at what he termed the "worthless life," in his own way coming close to Giorgio Agamben's analysis of *Homo sacer* as a life that can be killed with impunity.[128] "Nobody died," Mangs insisted, "as no one of any value died."[129] Mangs targeted everyday life. By killing or trying to kill people when they were at home, at work, commuting, working out, stopping for fast food, on their way to football practice, shopping, visiting the hospital, walking in the park, or going out dancing, he wanted to send a message to the black, Muslim, and Roma residents of the city that they were out of place and could not feel safe anywhere, at any time. To Mangs, the killings were political, "not personal." He hoped the victims and their relatives "would appreciate that." He had nothing against them, their husband, father, son, brother. He did not know them, nor was he interested in them – only in their death. "This was war. In wars, people die. I'm sorry, but that's the rule of the game."[130]

Mangs calculated how people would react to his killings. Following a murder or attempted murder, the detectives would map the victim's relations (family, friends, neighbors, colleagues, business contacts) and activities (work, political engagements, religious affiliations). Shooting a black, Muslim, or Roma victim in a stigmatized area with nonwhite residents would, Mangs concluded, cause the police to investigate other black, Muslim, and Roma persons in the community, thereby distributing the trauma further. Mangs correctly predicted that shooting and killing nonwhite people in Malmö would fuel media speculation of gang violence, black-on-black crime, drugs, and immigrant criminality, which would cast the blame on the victim and his kind, thereby magnifying the desired terror effect. In turn, this would strengthen white support for white radical nationalist parties and their tough-on-crime-and-immigration agenda and encourage violent assaults on nonwhite people and businesses. People in the target communities would feel unwanted and unprotected. Some would move; others would protest, their anger and complaints fueling further resentment from majority whites. To protect themselves, nonwhites would

---

[128] Agamben, 1998. [129] Mangs, Interview, June 17, 2014.
[130] Mangs, Interview, December 7, 2013; June 17, 2014.

organize vigilante groups that would scare white people, especially if they were to attack some white passerby, and hopefully kill him or her.

Through targeted killings, Mangs reasoned he could push the city off the cliff to civil war. He felt he played the city like a Kapellmeister his orchestra, with the police, the media, mainstream politicians, white nationalists, and nonwhite people playing their part at his command. He was the city manager, clearing urban space from polluting agents, spreading fear among the unwanted, and hastening the coming Ragnarök.[131]

Breivik calculated a nationalist war of liberation in three phases, ending in 2083 with total victory and the establishment of a monocultural white Christian European state. In the current phase, "spectacular operations" like July 22 would warn the cultural Marxists that the Knights Templar elite were coming for them, wherever they were, and would signal to Muslims to get out of Europe or die. Of course, the Knights Templar did not exist at the time of Breivik's writing, but he hoped to call it into existence by exemplary violence and the ensuing state repression against white nationalists.[132] As a service to future Crusader knights, Breivik included sections in his *2083* essay on rituals and ceremonies, chivalry ethics, practical advice, lone wolf rules, and how to acquire arms, produce chemical weapons, and build bombs.[133]

Breivik sought to awaken the white masses to the revolution. Mangs could think of no greater horror than doing anything together with such herd people. To him, the white masses were part of the problem. He projected that four-fifths of the white race (and everyone else) would die in the coming race war. Only the Aryan elite would survive and become the progenitors of the future race of Aryan supermen. Breivik foresaw "major bloodshed and millions of dead across the continent" in the cleansing race war, but wanted to spare the white race, only killing its traitors.[134] He spent hours making death lists and planning public executions of category A and B traitors, the cultural Marxist, feminist, and multicultural elites, for conspiring with the enemy to implement the "genocide against the (white) indigenous peoples of Europe."[135] Category C and D traitors, collaborators

[131] Mangs, Interview, December 13, 2013. [132] Breivik, 2011, pp. 1354ff.
[133] Breivik, 2011, pp. 847–853. [134] Breivik, 2011, pp. 742, 1353f.
[135] Breivik, 2011, p. 782.

of lesser importance, would be fined or spared, escaping death sentences to join the rest of the white masses in building the fascist state.

Mangs and Breivik read the same race war novels, including *Turner Diaries* and *Hunter*, and studied many of the same manuals. Breivik had been a member of the anti-Muslim, anti-immigrant Norwegian Progressive Party from 1997 to 2006; Peter Mangs had been a sympathizer of the ethnopluralist National Democrats and the conspiracy exposing Awake (*Vaken*).[136] When they joined the armed resistance, they left the organized scene and went underground, trying to abide by the books. Mangs and Breivik had no knowledge of each other before they were arrested. In fact, they became aware of each other only through their public trials. Incidentally, the first trial against Mangs in Malmö (May 14–October 2, 2012) occurred simultaneously to the trial against Breivik in Oslo (April 16– June 22, 2012). Breivik used the trial to propagate his views. He greeted the court with a fascist salute, was moved to tears when the prosecutor showed his YouTube film summarizing his manifesto, read two carefully prepared political declarations before the court, and hailed Mangs as a "brother-in-arms."

Peter Mangs put on a show as well, but in a very different manner. He demonstrated his contempt for the court, as he had during the police investigation. He did not explain himself – not to the enemy media, not to the court, not to the supporters he knew he had on social media. They had already received the message, the call to arms, the tactics, by him showing the way. Now, he showed how to behave if caught: no confession, no cooperation, no regrets, no sympathy for his victims. This was war; this was revolution. He was a self-created Aryan god, an *Übermensch*, a sovereign citizen, a free Aryan. The judge and prosecution were pawns of the system, legitimate only in the eyes of the masses, the herd animals, and were themselves part of the problem.

When I visited Mangs and Breivik in their respective maximum-security prisons, they both talked a lot about each other. Both saw their killings in terms of a "crusade" and complimented one another but also saw each other

---

[136] As part of his tactics, Mangs applied for membership in the Left Party but never paid the fees and hence did not become member.

as competitors. Who was the greatest resistance fighter? Whose tactics was the best? Who had achieved the most? Who was to be immortalized as a hero of the Aryan folk? "I have committed the most sophisticated, spectacular, and brutal political assault perpetuated by a militant nationalist in Europe since the end of the Second World War," Breivik proudly proclaimed.[137] "I know that he thinks he is the best," Mangs rebuked, "but those who will follow, follow me."[138]

Breivik was concerned that the parts of his *2083* manifesto in which he hails Israel and rebukes national socialism and anti-Semitism, the Swedish Resistance Movement, and (Norwegian) Vigrid[139] had been misunderstood, undermining his support among Nordic fascists. Simultaneously, he was annoyed. How stupid could they be? "It is enough there [in *2083*] to read behind the lines. Why do they think I quoted Madison Grant and incorporated texts by the BNP?" It was the same regarding being against anti-Semitism. "It's a *tactics*," Breivik exclaimed, "to reach the broader base who dislike Muslims." Israel is a "strategic ally."[140] Ideally, Jews should be in Israel and expand its territory at the expense of the Palestinians. Jews remaining in Europe need to join the white nationalist fight against Islam and Muslims. When that war is won, Europe has no space for Jews as Jews. As after the Spanish *Reconquista*, they must convert to Christianity or die. "My love for Israel," Breivik elaborated in a letter of 2014, "is limited to its capacity as deportation port for disloyal Jews."[141]

Breivik saw Mangs as second only to himself, "the greatest resistance fighter in Scandinavia since the Second World War until 22 July." Mangs used an "intelligent strategy," Breivik acknowledged. He "was a Swedish JPF" (Joseph Paul Franklin). "[He] applied the same tactics as in *Hunter*,

[137] Breivik, 2012. [138] Mangs, Interview, April 29, 2015.

[139] The Swedish Resistance Movement (est. 1997) became the Nordic Resistance Movement in 2016 with chapters in Sweden, Finland, Denmark, Norway, and Iceland and is to date the most visual national socialist organization in Scandinavia. Vigrid (est. 1998) is a Norse pagan fascist party in Norway.

[140] Breivik, Interview, June 19, 2014.

[141] Breivik, Letter to author, February 21, 2014; cf. Breivik, Letter to author, August 5, 2016.

a model which surely will inspire others to come." Breivik said he had written a letter to Mangs, but had not received any response. "Maybe they confiscated the letter," Breivik said. "I wrote that we were brothers in the same struggle. That he [Mangs] deserved respect," Breivik continued. "But I told him that he killed the wrong people." You "cannot blame blacks and Muslims for being savages, that's their nature." Go for the people who brought them here, who let them in. "Go for the traitors, the political class" – like he did on July 22.[142] The "preferred method" is a violent shock attack with limited forces, Breivik advises in *2083*. Employ "brutal and breath-taking operations" and "weapons of mass destruction." "Innocent people will die, in the thousands," but it is "better to kill too many than not enough." Breivik stressed an argument also repeated in the letter to Mangs; you need to "explain what you have done (in an announcement distributed prior to operation) and make certain that everyone understands that we, the free peoples of Europe, are going to strike again and again."[143]

"Good luck with that," Mangs commented; "1,500 pages of Breivik's writings. Who is going to read all of that?" Besides, to Mangs, the very idea of mobilizing the masses was distasteful. The masses had proven their worthlessness by allowing the problem to grow this big. Forget the masses; reach out to the small but determined Aryan elite who are not ashamed of their superiority and are willing to act against the enemy.

Mangs said he threw away the letter. He did not appreciate being reproached, and certainly not by Breivik. "He thinks he is the best; I can understand that," Mangs confided. "But really, what did he accomplish? He did that one thing, one day, and then got caught. Hit-and-die, or go direct to jail for the rest of your life. Quite hard to market, isn't it?" Much better to engage in low-intensity warfare. "Once you're done killing, you just walk away. You bury the guns, destroy them, throw them away, and no one has anything on you, no evidence, no nothing." Moreover, Breivik's operation was "really expensive," "mine affordable." "His way, you need to import lots of material, rent a safe house, get cars and uniforms. Mine? You buy a gun, a bicycle, and a pair of gloves." Breivik's method required "years of training" and preparation, "mine just a few days." Moreover, Breivik's way

[142] Breivik, Interview, June 19, 2014. [143] "Breivik, 2011, pp. 834, 847, 1362.

was mentally hard, Mangs said. "I've killed people. I know what it takes. To kill that many as he did, that's quite demanding. That makes me, based on my experience, to question how big the chances are that someone copies him. It's a far better chance that someone copies me. It's much easier, and much more effective to follow my way. What would happen if more people do what I did? If more people start to shoot? How would the police be able to handle that? If many copies me, copies my tactics, the system would collapse."[144]

Escalating Lone Wolf Violence

During Mangs' killing campaign, Malmö became branded as Sweden's Chicago, the capital of violence. Crime and immigration were key to a succession of Sweden Democrats (SD) election campaigns. Branding Malmö a "multicultural nightmare," a "no-go zone" overrun by violent Muslims, became a prominent feature of radical nationalist social media cross-nationally too, allowing white nationalists from Hungary to the USA to use Malmö and Sweden as a warning. Of course, there are no "no-go zones" in Sweden, and violent crime rates were declining. However, radical nationalist campaigns do not depend on empirical facts but an affective dimension, and the *image* of Malmö as a crime-ridden multicultural dystopia overshadowed actual crime statistics.[145]

In September, 2010, the SD was elected to parliament. For the first time in Swedish history, a party with national socialist origins made a breakthrough in national elections. That night, Mangs celebrated by manhunting. At the city hospital, he saw a group of Roma people waiting outside the emergency entrance. Hiding across the street, Mangs fired at a distance of twenty-five meters and disappeared into the night on his bicycle. From the news, he learned that a bullet had scored a three-centimeter-long rip along the top of one man's head. *An inch too high*, Mangs thought, and adjusted his new laser sight.[146]

The SD rose to become the largest party of white Swedish male voters. Its rise to prominence may be related to uncertainties about the future and

[144] Mangs, Interview, April 29, 2015; June 16, 2014. [145] BRÅ, 2012; 2015.
[146] Mangs, Interview, June 17, 2014; P4 Malmö, 2010.

widespread nostalgia for the society Sweden once was. Its geographical proximity to the Soviet Union had once allowed Sweden to build the Folk Home (*folkhem*), a semi-socialist system of social security, free education, universal medical and health care, affordable housing, and relative equality, achieved by gradual reform rather than communist revolution. Without the Soviet threat, Sweden went through a neoliberal restructuring of society, with the privatization of public goods, institutions, and services. Sweden went from being one of the world's most equal countries to a society with dramatically increasing class differences. Its growth in income inequality became the greatest among all OECD countries and, by 2018, Statistics Sweden reported the greatest gap between the country's rich and poor since measurement began.[147] Sweden transformed into one of the most segregated societies in the region. The basis of segregation is class, but as class distinctions covary with structural discrimination on the basis of racialized ethnicity, religion, and culture, they increasingly acquired a visual dimension, readily observable in the segregated urban areas of rich and poor. In reaction to these changes, white radical nationalists blamed immigration and pointed to visible minorities as signs of the betrayal of the political class, nostalgically envisioning a restored *folkhem* for white Swedish folks only.

The rise of white radical nationalism was accompanied by violence, directed at targets racialized as nonwhites. Violent assault, including arson, against mosques, homes for refugees, and Roma camps increased dramatically.[148] Anti-Muslim rhetoric entered mainstream conversations. An SD campaign video for the 2010 election featured a retired Swedish woman with a walker competing for state subsidies against a horde of niqab-clad women with carrycots. "On election day, you may choose to end immigration or her allowance. Vote Sweden Democrats."[149] In the 2014 national election campaign, SD party leader Jimmie Åkesson portrayed Islam as a "totalitarian ideology of total conquest," pointing to Islamic

---

[147] OECD, 2015; Andersson et al., 2009; Hogstedt et al., 2006; Grundström & Molina, 2016.

[148] The rise peaked between 2015 and 2018, with 52, 91, 74, and 55 arson or attempted arson attacks.

[149] "Pensionsbroms eller invandringsbroms," 2010.

State's slaughter of Christians in Iraq as a sign of what lies ahead for Christian Swedes. Åkesson performed the masculine warrior: "You can never kill us all. We are stronger than you think, and we will never flinch in the struggle against your barbarian, inhumane utopia." The SD won 13 percent of the national vote that election, achieving especially strong results in small-town areas with no or few Muslims.[150]

Anti-Muslim campaigns to burn down mosques, rip the veils off Muslim women, and kill vocal Muslims who publicly talked back caused widespread anxiety in the Muslim community.[151] In a 2018 survey of all Sunni, Shia, and Sufi congregations with prayer hall facilities in Sweden (a total of 167 mosques), I found that 59 percent had been exposed to physical assault, ranging from vandalism to arson, at least once, and 67 percent had received threats of various kinds; 45 percent had been attacked in the past year (2017) and a quarter of the respondents had experienced physical assault more than ten times.[152]

The fact that six out of ten mosques in Sweden have been attacked makes running and frequenting a mosque a high-risk venture. Among Islamic congregations, 26 percent have failed to find an insurance company willing to insure their facilities. In turn, this has opened a market for companies specializing in offering mosques and asylum centers insurance at high premiums, and high excess cost. For instance, when a sole perpetrator burned down the Imam Ali mosque at Järfälla in northern Stockholm, the congregation had to pay 1 million Swedish kronor before renovation could begin. Far from all violent crimes against mosques have been solved by the police; however, of those that have, we find white nationalist lone wolves among the perpetrators. For instance, when the great mosque in Borås, a textile-industrial city east of Gothenburg, was set ablaze on New Year's Eve 2017, the perpetrator operated on his own. He was caught by a gas station's security camera filling gasoline in a plastic bottle. He then climbed the mosque and poured the liquid onto the roof. An investigation revealed the perpetrator's dislike of Muslims and blacks and sympathy with the SD.[153]

---

[150] Åkesson, 2014. [151] Gardell, 2015b; 2018a. [152] Gardell, 2018a.

[153] Förundersökningsprotokoll, 5000-K63413-16, 2016; Gardell, 2018a; Gardell et al., 2017; Gardell, 2015b.

Interviews with Sweden Democrats show that they are familiar with lone wolf tactics and race war novels, including the American classics *Hunter* and *Turner Diaries*, as well as new Swedish-language fascist fiction.[154]

In the early fall of 2015, when many European countries locked their borders to refugees, Sweden stood by the right to seek asylum. "My Europe does not build walls," Prime Minister Stefan Löfven told a cheering Refugee Welcome mass rally in downtown southern Stockholm on September 6.[155] The SD was aghast. This was the "largest catastrophe" in modern history, nothing short of a "system collapse," party officials declared on October 15. Finding parliamentary methods "exhausted," SD representatives declared they would leave the parliament to encourage extra-parliamentary methods and campaign for a national referendum on immigration, as a last-minute effort to save the nation.[156]

On October 17, 2015, SD ideologue and MP Kent Ekeroth spoke at a national emergency meeting in a rainy Trelleborg before an audience of party sympathizers, assorted fascists, and local residents, addressing his audience as a "resistance" and the "spearheads" that would "retake our land." The speech was live-streamed and aired on YouTube and social media platforms. "The say that Swedish people have a long fuse," Ekeroth said, "but when the fuse has run its course, it will explode. And we'll show 'em! Time's up. Now it will explode!"[157]

A few hours later on October 17, an old school that had been rebuilt to receive refugees was burned to the ground in Kånna, south Sweden; on October 18, another school that had been set up to house refugees was set aflame in Onsala; on October 20, an arson attack was attempted at a residential home for refugees in Munkedal; on October 21, a planned refugee home in Upplands Väsby was vandalized, but the attempted arson failed; on October 23, a house ready to receive refugees was burned to the ground; on October 24, the residential home for refugees in Munkedal was set aflame again; on October 26, a clinic for refugee children with disabilities was burned down; on October 27, a home that had been set up to house

[154] Gardell, 2021. [155] Löfven, 2015. [156] Sverigedemokraterna, 2015.
[157] Ekeroth, 2015.

refugee minors was set aflame by using Bibles to start the fire; on October 28, two refugee homes were attacked with explosives and then set on fire. The coming month would look the same. In the midst of this wave of violence, the Sweden Democrats found reason to publish the addresses of planned housing facilities for refugees, citing the people's right to know and the freedom of expression.[158]

The wave of violence also materialized in a lethal lone wolf attack. On October 22, five days after Ekeroth's call for action to save the nation, twenty-six-year-old Anton Lundin Pettersson, who "liked" the SD campaign on social media and signed the SD petition for a referendum, took action. Draped in a long black coat, a German Second World War helmet, a black face mask, and a Viking sword replica, he walked into Kronan elementary school in Trollhättan and stabbed students Ahmed Hassan, Nazir Azmo, Wahid Kosa Mohammad, and David Issa, and member of school personnel Lavin Eskander, three of them to death. Lundin Pettersson had not studied at that school, did not know his victims, and most likely had not met them before. Security cameras and witness reports indicate that his victims were randomly selected for looking nonwhite and non-Swedish. An investigation of Lundin Pettersson's computer found lots of fascist material – memes, films, texts, pictures, and content by influencers, including the Golden One, one of Sweden's more renowned contributions to the white nationalist manosphere.[159]

"I can't stand this f* communist country no more," Lundin Pettersson wrote in his farewell letter. "They don't give a damn about our elders who built this country, while Muslims and scum are patted on the head for raping our beautiful nation. You made me do this. The blood is on your hands."[160]

---

[158] Gardell et al., 2017; "Detta har hänt: Flera attacker på kort tid," 2015.

[159] Förundersökningsprotokoll, Dnr 5000-K1353421-15, 2015; *Uppgifter som ej ingår i FU-protokoll,* Dnr 5000-K1353421-15, 2015; 2016; GMs mobil, Dnr 5000-K1353421-15, 2016; Förhör, Dnr 5000-K1353421-15, 2015; Förundersökningsprotokoll AM-144882–15, 2015; Anmälan, Dnr 5000-K1353421-15, 2015.

[160] Lundin Pettersson, *Avskedsbrev.* Dnr 5000-K1353421-15, 2015.

White nationalists celebrated. "May the Sword of Lord Anton Lundin Pettersson save Sweden," said a Facebook page named "Anton Lundin Pettersson just defended his country." His YouTube account, "HipHopDestroyer666," was loaded with salutes, praise, and condemnation, naming him an idiot or a hero. He was a "Deus vult anon topkek" (a crusading anonymous white super-fascist). "Your ancestors would be proud. You protected your realm and the blood of your people like you could. They've kept a warm place in Valhalla for you."[161]

Breaking the Rules

A basic rule for lone wolves is to go under the radar. The man – so far it is mostly men – who decides to join the resistance as a one-man army should shun organized white nationalist organizations and activities; abstain from revealing his opinions, except through avatars or anonymous social media interventions; melt into the general population; and not tell anyone of violent crimes planned or committed. These are simple, reasonable rules, but hard to follow, especially if you join the cause to become a male warrior hero.

Let me illustrate by looking at Peter Mangs, who saw himself as a Nietzschean Superman, an Aryan god, a Hero of the Sagas, who should be commemorated in the songs of the blood. Besides heroic fascist fiction, a source of inspiration feeding his warrior dreams was American movies portraying the lone avenger; he named among his favorites *Death Wish*, *The Bourne Identity*, *Falling Down*, *James Bond*, and *Braveheart*. However, the action hero has the audience as witness. Mangs had no audience, and could not tell anyone about his heroic accomplishments. Following the euphoria after the first murder, Mangs fell into despair. The world outside his apartment window continued unabated as if nothing had happened. Surely, it confirmed his conviction that his victim, the Iranian-born retiree, was a worthless life, possible to kill with impunity. However, it also sent Mangs into a downward spiral of existential inquiry to which he had no answer. If a tree falls in a forest and no animal is there to hear it, does it make a sound? If no one knows that something happened, did it happen?

---

[161] "Discussion," Anton Lundin Pettersson, YouTube.

Does the hero exist without witness? He had to tell, had to take credit. A few days later, he called his father Rudolf and told him everything. Was he sure nobody had seen him? his father wanted to know. Mangs regularly updated his father on his series of racist killings, but each time he was disappointed by his father's practical response, and it was only after Mangs had been convicted that Rudolf praised his son as a "forerunner" who would "one day stand statue." Mangs had to enroll other witnesses. First, he told a childhood friend and everyday racist; later, he let a hardcore national socialist and admirer of Oskar Dirlewanger know, and finally got the acclaim he needed. Eventually, both friends would cooperate with the police when Mangs was finally arrested.[162]

5 White Genocide and the Great Replacement

On March 15, 2019, minutes before leaving home to commit the massacre of mosque attendees in Christchurch, Brenton Tarrant posted a manifesto, *The Great Replacement*, on 8chan's "pol" board, where a section of the alt-right online community gather.[163] This was his way to alert the white community to what was going on, to call from the rooftops.

At the core of the manifesto is Tarrant's conviction that the white race is dying. If nothing is *done*, it will be forever too late. Two factors, he writes, determine the outcome: reproduction and immigration. The first refers to the white nations' aging populations and falling birthrates, the second to the alleged "mass-invasion" of nonwhite people to "white lands" in the global North: Europe, America, Australia, and New Zealand. The "native" white population is being "replaced" by racialized others in a "white genocide" program that will reduce white people to an oppressed minority in "their own lands," he argues.[164] Becoming a minority is not a good idea, Tarrant warns. "Minorities are never treated well, do not become one."[165]

---

[162] Rudolf Mangs, Interview, February 3, 2015; Peter Mangs, Interview, November 10, 2013; December 8, 2013; January 11, 2014; Förhör med vittnen, 2010–12–02; 2011–01–11, Dnr 1200-K163215-09.

[163] Tarrant, 2019a. [164] Tarrant, 2019a, pp. 4, 52. [165] Tarrant, 2019a, p. 52.

Tarrant calls on white youth to "not go gentle into that good night," but raise their swords. "Radical, explosive action is the only desired, and required, response to an attempted genocide."[166] Similarly, Mangs and Breivik motivated their killings as necessary to save the white race from extermination, as did other lone wolves. To many observers, these motivations point to the perpetrators' delusionary minds, to them being lone nuts, schizophrenic, paranoid. However, the theory of the Great Replacement and the fears of a white genocide have a long genealogy that can be traced through intertextual references, using Tarrant's manifesto as a starting point.

The Great Replacement

With the 2017 Unite the Right rally in Charlottesville, Virginia, and its mantra "You will not replace us," and the 2019 Christchurch massacre, mainstream media discovered the Great Replacement theory.

In journalistic accounts, the theory was widely attributed to French "identitarian" philosopher Renaud Camus (b. 1946).[167] In his 2011 book *Le grand remplacement*, Camus claims that France is currently being occupied by Muslim and African invaders who seek to replace the native French population according to a masterplan of a shadowy "replacist power" (*pouvoir remplaciste*) and corrupt traitors in the French establishment. To Camus, the French situation is but part of a *remplacisme global* by which the peoples of the world are remade into identical and replaceable units of production, bereft of their aboriginal identities, cultures, and histories. Of course, Camus' main concern is the alleged invasion of France, a malady for which he has a remedy: forced "remigration."[168]

Camus' conspiracy theory of a hidden agent scheming to substitute the French population with alien "Muslim and African" others rejects the republican definition of the French nation – a French person is a citizen of France – in favor of a racial definition of blood and essence, stipulating that a Muslim born in France to French citizens who are Muslim is Muslim,

---

[166] Tarrant, 2019a, p. 34. "Do not go gentle into that good night," poem by Dylan Thomas, quoted in Tarrant, 2019a, p. 2.

[167] Charlton, 2019; Chatterton Williams, 2017; McAuley, 2019. [168] Camus, 2012.

not French. Hence, there seems to be an inborn quality of alienating *Muslimness* that makes the newborn life an eternal stranger in his or her country of birth.

Blood determines identity. "The idea that all it takes for a Han Chinese man to become German is to be born on German soil is as insane as a German born on Mars becoming a Martian," Tarrant states in his manifesto. Blood entitles; blood defines. A Europe without Europeans is not Europe at all, the mantra goes. European is something that you either are or are not; it is not something you may become or aspire to be – not if you are of the wrong blood. That holds true for your children and their children, too. There can be no alternative, blood nationalists insist. Not if we want to preserve Europe. "When non-Europeans are considered Europe, then there is no Europe at all."[169]

Camus' work is influential among white identitarians in Europe, and his name has occasionally been picked up in American alt-right conversations, including the *Counter-Currents* podcast with Greg Johnson, and the writings of Jared Taylor.[170] However, despite the fact that Tarrant's manifesto bears the same title as Camus' book, there is no indication that he read it, or even knew it existed, possibly because it had not been translated into English. Tarrant says he heard many "stories and rumors" about the non-European invasion of France that he found to be "true" when traveling there,[171] but does not cite Camus as a source. While Tarrant and Camus share the assumption that blood transmits culture, religion, and identity, and the conviction that "native" Europeans are being replaced by non-Europeans, they were both informed by other currents with a long history of circulation.

Camus writes in the tradition of the French Nouvelle Droit, not least Guillaume Faye, and Bat Ye'or's Eurabia theory of a conspiracy to Islamize France. *Le grand remplacement* is indebted to the French fascist René Binet (1913–1957), whose *Théorie du Racisme* (1950) argues that capitalism promotes race-mixing and the "false doctrine" of equality to produce an inferior race exploitable as a workforce. Influential to Camus was also *Le*

---

[169] Tarrant, 2019a, p. 62. [170] Johnson & Morgan, 2019; Taylor, 2018.
[171] Tarrant, 2019a, p. 8.

Camp des Saints, the "prophetic" 1973 novel by Jean Raspail (b. 1925) on the dying Western civilization, drowning in the tidal wave of Third World immigration, and the "Rivers of Blood" speech by Enoch Powell, both classic references in the wider white radical nationalist landscape.[172]

White Genocide

Important to Tarrant was the work of white nationalist David Lane (1938–2007), who coined the "14 Words" – "We must secure the existence of our people and a future for white children" – which Tarrant scribbled on his AR-15 and quoted three times in *The Great Replacement*.[173]

Lane originally published the 14 Words in his 1988 *White Genocide Manifesto*. Written in prison, and circulating as a handout, it had a modest reception at the time. That changed when David Lane married the entrepreneurial Katja Lane (*née* Maddox), who built his reputation as the Caged Revolutionary, unjustly imprisoned for seeking to end the extermination of the white race. Together with artist Ron McVan, the Lanes launched the Idaho-based Odinist Wotansvolk ministry and the 14 Word Press to disseminate his writings, including *White Genocide Manifesto*, *88 Precepts*, *Revolution by Number 14*, *The Mystery Religions*, *Wodensson in Verse*, *Auto-Biographical Portrait of the Life of David Lane*, and *Deceived, Damned & Defiant: The Revolutionary Writings of David Lane*.

When the *White Genocide Manifesto* was reprinted in 1994, its publication came at the dawn of the Internet revolution, and the 14 Words quickly became a household concept across the worldwide white web. To Lane, that was hardly a coincidence. Whites were the originators of every major technological innovation, from cars to space carriers. Now, white ingenuity had invented the Internet and global communication technologies to make sure that knowledge about the ongoing white genocide reached ever corner of the white world, allowing the notoriously factious white nationalists to center their effort on the one thing that really matters: racial survival.[174]

To Lane, it was the USA – not France or Europe – that was at the center of the Great Replacement/white genocide drama. According to Lane, the

---

[172] Raspail, 1973; Powell, 1969. [173] Tarrant, 2019a, pp. 7, 18f.
[174] Lane, Interview, November 12, 1996.

USA was from its very inception part of the plan to exterminate the white race and grind together the diverse cultures of the world into one mongrel race of soulless and interchangeable production units, as evidenced by its motto, *E Pluribus Unum* (one out of many). As a superpower, the USA was to use its military might to destroy every white territorial initiative on the globe, as evidenced when it intervened to end Germany's effort to "defend the race" in the Second World War. Following the war, the borders of Europe opened to invading "Moors and Mongols" to terminate the white race, as "racial integration is genocide for the White race through miscegenation." Time is running out. "The life of a race is in the wombs of its women." Only 2 percent of the earth's population are white women, whom antiwhite forces encourage to stop breeding white children. "Death of a race is eternal," Lane warns, urging white men to do whatever is necessary to "preserve the beauty of their women and a future for White children."[175]

The Passing of the Great Race

Lane was inspired by earlier efforts to secure the survival of the white (Nordic) race,[176] notably Americans Madison Grant and Lothrop Stoddard, and German National Socialism.

Madison Grant (1865–1937), lawyer, conservationist, and director of the American Eugenics Society, and Lothrop Stoddard (1883–1950), historian, author, and Ku Klux Klan consultant, called for the preservation from extinction of the "Nordic stock" by applied eugenics, sterilization programs, and restricted immigration. They furthered Victorian concerns of "racial suicide" as "clannish" immigrants (Irish and Italian) with alien "race, blood, and religion" were allowed to enter the country and produce "home-grown foreigners" at a time when "native" (white) American fertility rates were dwindling.[177] In the race-blood-religion constellation at work here, white Protestant and Catholic Americans were separated as two distinct "races" of different blood, essence, and features.

---

[175] Lane, 1988; Lane, Interview, November 12, 1996; Lane, 1994b; 1995a; 1995b; 1996.

[176] Gardell, 2003. [177] King & Ruggles, 1990; Bennet, 1995.

In *The Passing of the Great Race* (1916), Grant argues that "Native Americans," a term he reserves for white Nordic Americans, are an endangered species, pushed off their lands and extinguished in the melting pot. Due to industrialization and urbanization, "Native Americans" are being crowded out and outbred by "alien people," "the Slovak, the Italian, the Syrian, and the Jew,"[178] who are "whites of a different color."[179]

Whiteness, of course, is not given by nature but determined by context and defined by law, as shown by Ian Haney López.[180] Of the four categories Grant excludes from whiteness, two (the Slovak and the Italian) would later be included when the borders of whiteness were renegotiated 100 years later, while the whiteness of the other two categories (the Syrian and the Jew) remain contested to this day.

In 2020, the Syrian may be included as white if Christian, but the Jew still finds his existence debatable. While some radical white nationalists (including Robert Spencer, Jared Taylor, and Anders Behring Breivik) see Jews as potential allies and admire efforts to make Israel a Jewish ethnostate, other white nationalists hold Jews as the hidden hand behind the Great Replacement, as illustrated in the chant "Jews will not replace us."

In other respects, Grant's (1916) words ring as if published in the twenty-first century. "These immigrants [i.e., the Slovak, the Italian, the Syrian, and the Jew] adopt the language of the native [i.e., white] American," Grant wrote. "[T]hey wear his clothes; they steal his name; and they are beginning to take his women, but they seldom adopt his religion or understand his ideals." The "Native American," Grant laments, allows himself to be "elbowed out of his own home," "abandoning to these aliens the land which he conquered and developed."[181]

Grant argues that the melting pot eradicates whiteness and produces inferior races suitable for industrial production but incapable of self-governance. Superiority is to Grant a fine, almost ephemeral, quality, easily contaminated, that needs to be kept separate or suffer death by contact.[182]

In *The Rising Tide of Color* (1920), Lothrop Stoddard positions the "white world" at the "crossroads of life and death."[183] Writing from the

---

[178] Grant, 1916, p. 43. [179] Jacobson, 1998. [180] López, 2006.
[181] Grant, 1916, p. 43. [182] Grant, 1916, p. 13. [183] Stoddard, 1920, p. 196.

vantage point of unprecedented white imperial power, Stoddard points out that the white race still is a minority, everywhere surrounded by inferior races.[184]

The white Nordic race – "the best of all human breeds" – had been severely decimated in the First World War as the best men on both sides had been Nordics. "From a racial standpoint, indeed, Armageddon was a Nordic civil war."[185] In addition, the Nordic suffered more than any other race from European industrialization and urbanization, processes inducing the "racial displacements" of (superior white) Nordic men by people of (inferior white) Alpine and Mediterranean, (Asiatic) Levantine, and Jewish races.[186]

In North America, the Nordic race was "deluged by the truly alien hordes of the European east and south" that became a menace to the race and soul of the colonial stock, which they "*replaced*, not reinforced."[187] If the "influx of inferior kindred stocks" was bad, Stoddard warns, imagine the effect of the coming tide of color. "The whole white race is exposed, immediately or ultimately," Stoddard concludes, to the "final replacement or absorption by the teeming colored races."[188]

Alarmed, Congress passed the Emergency Quota Act of 1921 and the Immigration Act of 1924 to favor immigration from Northern and Western Europe at the expense of migrants from Eastern and Southern Europe, in addition to already existing laws excluding Indigenous American, African, Asian, and Chinese people from citizenship, along with anarchists, beggars, and various classes of disabled people.

All of this greatly impressed Adolf Hitler, who kept a well-read and much-quoted copy of Grant's *The Passing of the Great Race* in his private library.[189] Grant was required reading among German race theorists, and the German translation of his 1933 *Conquest of a Continent* was recommended by Joseph Goebbels, Reichsminister of public enlightenment and propaganda. The eugenics program of the Third Reich and the Nuremberg Laws of 1935 were to a considerable extent modelled on the American

---

[184] Stoddard, 1920, pp. 9, 196. [185] Stoddard, 1920, p. 183.

[186] Stoddard, 1920, pp. 163–165. [187] Stoddard, 1920, p. 263, italics original.

[188] Stoddard, 1920, p. 298. [189] Ryback, 2010, pp. 94–115; Regal, 2004, p. 334.

eugenic programs and US racial law[190] and Alfred Rosenberg, who was personally acquainted with Lothrop Stoddard, took the term *Untermensch* from the latter's 1922 work *The Revolt Against Civilization: The Menace of the Under-Man.*[191]

Lebensraum

Hitler sought to return the Aryan race to its imagined former greatness. He believed that times were dire. Jewish bolshevism threatened to exterminate the Aryan race, and with it the entire human civilization, as Hitler wrote in *Mein Kampf*; "every manifestation of human culture, every product of art, science, and technical skill" is "the product of the Aryan creative power." Should the archetypes of man perish, "all that makes the earth beautiful will descend with them into the grave." Should the Aryans disappear, a "profound darkness will descend on earth; within a few thousand years human culture will vanish and the world will become a desert."[192]

To avert the imminent threat and pave the way for national rebirth, Hitler aimed at using the powers of the national socialist state to destroy Jewish bolshevism, reassert Aryan culture, implement programs of positive and negative eugenics, and secure sufficient *Lebensraum* (living space) for the *Volk* to thrive.

Lebensraum was a key concept within national socialism, but had been used to legitimize territorial conquest and settler colonialism before. In 1901, geographer Friedrich Ratzel defined *Lebensraum* as "the geographical surface area required to support a living species at its current population size and mode of existence."[193] Its exact borders were relative to the species' adaptability. Evolutionary success meant spatial expansion, as a superior *Volk* migrates and explores new territories to conquer and cultivate. Securing *Lebensraum* had become a motif for establishing German overseas colonies in Africa and Asia, and for fighting the Great War. With national socialism, the quest for *Lebensraum* returned to the fore.

[190] Kühl, 2012; Whitman, 2017. [191] Stoddard, 1922.
[192] Hitler, 1939, pp. 182–183.
[193] Cited in Smith, 1980, pp. 51–68; Burgdörfer, 1934.

According to the organic conception of race and *Volk* in national socialist political philosophy, *Lebensraum* was conceived as the living space or breathing space necessary for racial survival and prosperity. To thrive, the organic *Volk* must have sufficient *Lebensraum*, cleared of competing life-forms. Hitler admired the British Empire, which had conquered so much space for the white British *Volk* all over the world. Yet, he shelved his original plan to retake Germany's "place in the sun" (i.e., its overseas colonies), which had been lost in the Great War. Hitler sought instead to emulate the white American conquest of the West by establishing a colonial empire on the continent in which it was the dominant power.

The conquest of the German East (*der deutsche Osten*) was analogous to the conquest of the American West, the equivalent of what white Americans called "Manifest Destiny": a racially superior people expands at the expense of inferior peoples doomed by Nature to obliteration.[194] "Here in the East a similar process will repeat itself for a second time as in the conquest of America," Hitler said. The Volga will be "our Mississippi," and "Europe – and not America – will be the land of unlimited possibilities."[195]

To Hitler, the conquest of the East was a colonial war of annihilation (*Vernichtungskrieg*) between incompatible life-forms (fascists versus communists; Aryans versus Jews), in which the prize was the privilege of life itself. Speaking to the top officers under his command, Hitler said they could not "leave this urgent task to future generations."[196]

Crusades and Reconquista

Why would Brenton Tarrant seek the remedy for shrinking white birthrights and *Lebensraum* by massacring mosque attendees in New Zealand? Much like Stoddard, Tarrant found the peril of the white folk universal. New Zealand was not his original choice; he only went there to plan and train. While there, however, he realized that an attack in Christchurch would draw attention to the "truth" that Europeans had no refuge anywhere. "The invaders were in all of our lands, even the remotest areas of the world."[197]

---

[194] Horseman, 1981. [195] Fritz, 2018, p. 126.

[196] Fritz, 2018, p. 125; Halder, 1963, p. 336f; Hillgruber, 1989; Kakel, 2011.

[197] Tarrant, 2019a, p. 11.

Tarrant did not hate people of other cultures, or so he claims. He had spent years traveling abroad, everywhere having been "treated wonderfully, often as a guest and even as a friend."[198] Reiterating ethnopluralist rhetoric, Tarrant posits that the Christchurch massacre was not an attack on diversity, but made "in the name of diversity." The bloodbath was intended to encourage the peoples of the world to stay in their assigned places, "diverse, separate, unique, undiluted."[199] Should they drift out of place, however, they could justifiably be killed.

But why Muslims? Tarrant insists that it was not personal. He did not kill the particular Muslims in Christchurch because of anything they had done; he did not even know their names. He killed them because of who they were: Muslims in Christchurch. He did not hate Muslims "living in their homelands."[200] Being in Christchurch by choice or birth made Muslims "invaders" and marked them for death. Their Muslimness made them aliens; their being in New Zealand made them out of place. Muslims born there were eternal strangers in their land of birth, as blood, not territory, defines who you are, and where your home is. Inspired by Breivik, Tarrant felt entitled to act as "jury, judge, and executioner" on behalf of the "indigenous [white] people" and kill the invaders.[201]

Tarrant is a Millennial born in October 1990. He grew up in the post-Cold War era after the Soviet Union had collapsed and as Islam and Muslims gradually were reinstalled as representing that which the West was not: the East. He was eleven years old on September 11, 2001 and came to age with the ensuing War on Terror. He knew of no world in which Muslims were not the racialized other; he had yet to live one day without media representing Muslims negatively. Targeting Muslims was the obvious thing to do: "They are the most despised group of invaders in the West," Tarrant observed, "attacking them receives the greatest level of support."[202]

Tarrant alleges he did "contact the reborn Knights Templar for a blessing in support of the attack."[203] By then, Breivik had been in solitary confinement for seven years. He was not allowed to see anyone but his

---

[198] Tarrant, 2019a, p. 12. [199] Tarrant, 2019a, p. 14. [200] Tarrant, 2019a, p. 12
[201] Breivik, 2011, p. 830. [202] Tarrant, 2019a, p. 21f. [203] Tarrant, 2019a, p. 0.

lawyer, his mother, and me, a researcher; with few exceptions, all of his correspondence was confiscated. When Breivik launched the Norwegian Fascist Party and Nordic League (later renamed Nordic State) he was denied permission to communicate with sympathizers and failed to challenge the restrictions in court. Had Tarrant and Breivik been in contact, the Norwegian authorities would certainly have read their correspondence.[204]

Tarrant's claim to have received the blessing of Breivik was likely a flirt with Breivik's pose of having been initiated as Justiciar Knight Sigurd the Crusader of the Knights Templar (*Pauperes commilitones Christi Templique Solomonici*) at the London ceremony in which the order allegedly was refounded in 2002.[205]

Breivik's Knights Templar story seems neither hyperbole, nor delusionary, nor true, but instead a meant-to-be clever, edgy, and entertaining case of twilight talk, traversing the space between true and untrue in a manner typical of the digital culture of the white nationalist landscape, which plays with irony and satire to "hide in plain sight."[206]

Breivik's and Tarrant's romance with the crusading knights evokes a long tradition. The Knights Templar (1119–1312) have been part of the Western esoteric tradition since the 1700s, and of popular culture since Sir Walter Scott's 1820 epos *Ivanhoe*, when the terms "crusade'" and "crusader" were coined for what in medieval times had been termed "peregrination" (pilgrimage), and *crucesignatus* (someone signed by the cross).[207]

Crusading knights have been a feature in the white nationalist landscape ever since, as evidenced by the Knights of the Ku Klux Klan, and saw a revival when Muslims returned to the fore as the archenemy of the West after the collapse of communism. When Tarrant inserts a lengthy quote by Pope Urban II calling for Holy War against the "impious race of the Saracen" (the Muslims) at the Council of Clermont in 1095, his writing is not odd, but familiar.[208]

---

[204] *Oslo tingrett,* 2012; Oslo Borgarting Lagmanssrett, 2017; Breivik, Interview, June 19, 2014; Breivik, Letter to author, October 20, 2015; August 5, 2016.

[205] Breivik, 2011, pp. 827, 842, 1380f, 1416f. [206] May & Feldman, 2019.

[207] Markowski, 1984, pp. 157–165; Gaposchkin, 2017. [208] Tarrant, 2019a, p. 26.

"The crusades refuse to remain in the past," observe Mike Horswell and Akil N. Awan in their study of the ways in which crusading rhetoric frames and justifies political violence in the present.[209] Reverberating in the present is also the Iberian *Reconquista*.

Born out of nineteenth-century Spanish nationalism, the concept of the *Reconquista* is used to project the construct of a Christian Spanish nation back to the times of the Romans and Visigoths, albeit that the two periods were "interrupted" by almost 800 years of Muslim rule. It encompasses all the events that led to the end of *al-Andalus*, the "Muslim Spain," and the establishment of "Christian Spain" as "true Spain": wars and battles; forced conversions; edicts banning Muslim clothing, literature, and festivals; torture interrogations of suspected crypto-Jews and Muslims; campaigns of ethnic cleansing. Above all, it signifies the 1492 edict to expel all the Jews, and the 1609 expulsion of all the "Moriscos" (people of "Muslim background") from the Kingdom.[210]

The concept of *Reconquista* has proven politically powerful. It was utilized by General Franco to signify the effort to rid the country of democracy, liberalism, egalitarianism, socialism, and anarchism. In current white nationalist usage, the concept is used as a call for purging "white territories" from the Muslim and leftist/liberal presence, including the effort of the *Reconquista Germanica* to "reclaim" cyberspace from cultural Marxism, feminism, antiracism, and "social justice warriors."[211]

Allusions to the *Reconquista* abound in the white nationalist landscape. Besides references to the *Reconquista* in white nationalist speeches, conferences, projects, books, music, and gaming culture, there are numerous online retailers vending *Reconquista* products such as artwork, coffee mugs, gifts, framed prints, banners, T-shirts, hoodies, baby clothes, maternity clothes, caps, hats, bags, and flip-flops.

"There will only be two options" for white Europeans, Guillaume Faye says: "our historic disappearance, or a *Reconquista*."[212] "Muslims will be expelled from Europe yet again," Breivik asserts, "after major bloodshed

[209] Horswell & Awan, 2020. [210] Silva, 2020. [211] Ebner, 2020.
[212] Faye, 2016; cf. Holland et al., 2016; Faye, 2011; 2019.

and millions of dead across the continent."[213] Tarrant echoes: "Remove the invaders, retake Europe."[214]

Eco-Fascism

Brenton Tarrant defines himself an "ethno-nationalist eco-fascist" who wants "ethnic autonomy" and the "preservation of nature."[215]

Positioned beyond the trope of national socialism as a "philosophy of nature," eco-fascists promote a radically green (state-centered or tribal) fascism in which the organic white race/culture/folk is holistically integrated into a natural environment that can only be saved through a sharp reduction in pollution and overpopulation. Combined with ethnopluralism, eco-fascists typically argue that different races/cultures/folk by nature belong to their distinct habitats of origin, which they are obliged to protect from invasive species.

Eco-fascism traces its lineage back the *Völkish* rejection of industrialization and urbanization as devastating to *Volk* and wilderness, and its romance with simple peasant life and forest culture. Of course, the main threat was "Jewish" industrialism, capitalism, and bolshevism, seen as rootless, urban, and exploitative of nature.[216]

In the Third Reich, a "green dimension" was reflected in the thoughts of Heinrich Himmler, Alfred Rosenberg, Rudolf Hess, Walter Darré, and Hermann Göring. Himmler was a vegetarian who preferred organic food, holistic medicine, and experimented with biodynamic farming. Rosenberg saw the future of the race and soul in the Nordic farmer cultivating the *Lebensraum* freed for him.[217] Argentina-born Walter Darré, Reich peasant leader and minister of agriculture, popularized the slogan *Blut und Boden* (blood and soil) and promoted "farming according to the laws of life" (*lebensgesetzliche Landbauweise*), that is, biodynamic farming.[218] As master of German forests, Göring introduced the unprecedented National Nature

---

[213] Breivik, 2011, p. 741. [214] Tarrant, 2019a, p. 50.

[215] Tarrant, 2019a, pp. 16, 18.

[216] Zimmerman & Toulouse, 2016; Biehl & Staudenmaier, 2011; Staudenmaier, 2001.

[217] Rosenberg, 1939. [218] Staudenmaier, 2013.

Protection Act (*Reichsnaturschutzgesetz*) of 1935 to safeguard the wildlife, natural monuments, and forests of the Reich.[219]

Of course, the environmental policies of the Third Reich were in place to serve national socialism's major objectives. "The concept of Blood and Soil gives us the moral right to take back as much land in the East as is necessary to establish a harmony between the body of our Volk and its geopolitical space," Darré emphasized.[220] As noted by Simon Schama in *Landscape and Memory*, "Exterminating millions of lives was not at all incompatible with passionate protection for millions of trees."[221]

Contemporary eco-fascists may overstate the ecological significance of historic national socialism but see in its genocidal practice the measures necessary to save the planet. Unsurprisingly, white eco-fascists point at racialized others as the problem. "We Europeans are one of the groups that are not overpopulating the world," Tarrant states. "The invaders are the ones overpopulating the world. Kill the invaders, kill the overpopulation and by doing so save the environment."[222]

Inspired by Tarrant was Patrick Crusius, who posted his manifesto, *The Inconvenient Truth*, on 8chan before entering a Walmart in El Paso, Texas, on August 3, 2019 and massacring twenty-three people he took (and mistook) for Hispanics. Like Tarrant, Crusius claimed he had killed in order to preserve "racial diversity." "I am simply defending my country from cultural and ethnic replacement brought on by an invasion."[223]

Crusius took the title of his manifesto from Al Gore's Oscar-winning documentary on the planetary environment crisis. "The decimation of the environment is creating a massive burden for future generations," Crusius writes. "Corporations are heading the destruction of our environment by shamelessly overharvesting resources," encouraging "consumer culture," and allowing the entry of millions of migrants. The only remedy is to "decrease the number of people in America using resources. If we can get rid of enough people, then our way of life can become more sustainable."[224]

[219] Lekan, 1999; Bramwell, 1985; Biehl & Staudenmaier, 2011; Stephens, 2001; Baranowski & Nolzen, 2018; Lee & Wilke, 2015.

[220] Quoted in Kakel, 2011. [221] Schama, 1996. [222] Tarrant, 2019a, p. 22.

[223] Crusius, 2019. [224] Crusius, 2019.

The reference to Al Gore highlights the ways in which the green politics that for decades have been thought of as a province of the political left may be constitutive to the worldview of a white radical nationalist. Of course, as indicated by the green dimension of historical national socialism, this is hardly surprising. Nature is a social construct that is gendered (Mother Nature, who is nurturing, vindictive, etc.), classed (the wilderness is transformed into a space for recreation industry), sexualized (barren wasteland, fertile soil, impenetrable forests), and racialized (peoples of nature/ peoples of culture), as discussed by Johan Hultgren. In *Border Walls Gone Green*, Hultgren shows how anti-immigration groups have been able to "expand their alliances beyond the far right while still maintaining the support of [white] nativists."[225]

From the 1970s to the 1990s, Sierra Club official John Tanton sought to mainstream the argument that migration and overpopulation were the root causes of environmental collapse by establishing a network of "centrist-left" groups for "immigration reform," including the Federation for American Immigration Reform and the Center for Immigration Studies, specifically warning of the devastating impact of Latinos. In 1994, his Social Contract Press published Jean Raspail's novel *Le Camp des Saints* in English (*The Camp of the Saints*), which came to influence the Great Replacement theory, and in the same year Tanton co-authored *The Immigration Invasion*, which summarized the conservationist call to protect nature from invasive species.[226]

Hence, we have a green dimension in radical nationalist thought articulated by groups such as the British National Party, Jobbik, the True Finns, the Nordic Resistance Movement,[227] and a white racist current in "progressive" political thought, environmentalism, and conservationism. After all, Madison Grant was an American progressive who sought to preserve the Nordic race, but also the redwood forests and the American bison. He cofounded the Sierra Club and the Wildlife Conservation Society and helped to establish nature preserves, including the Denali, Olympic, Everglades, and Glacier National Parks.[228]

---

[225] Hultgren, 2015.

[226] Cagle, 2019; Hultgren, 2015; Lutton & Tanton, 1994; Rohe, 2002.

[227] Forchtner, 2019. [228] Spiro, 2009.

To Tarrant, racism and environmentalism are two sides of the same coin. "Continued immigration into Europe is environmental warfare and ultimately destructive to nature itself," Tarrant states. "Each ethnicity was melded by their own environment and if they are to be protected so must their own environments."[229]

That could hardly be achieved by nonviolent means. "A gradual change is never going to achieve victory," Tarrant argues. Change will come when the system collapses from its internal contradictions. "Therefore, we must destabilize and discomfort society wherever possible."[230] Tarrant thought civil war was bound to commence in the USA and that it could use a helping hand. The spark, he suggests, would come in Texas, where the replacement of whites would soon hit its apogee and remaining white folks would realize what had happened.[231]

Of course, Crusius wanted to be that spark.

6 Digital Fascism and the Gamification of the Lone Wolf

The previous analysis of Tarrant's *Great Replacement* manifesto arrives at the conclusion that it does not really contain anything new, but rather stands forth as a recasting and repetition of ideas and perspectives that have been around for a long time: white entitlement to land, resources, and privileges; the connection between white people and the territory they claim as theirs – blood and soil; race and space; the right to sufficient *Lebensraum* for the white race to thrive at the expense of others; the curious perception of the white race as an organic entity of supreme strength and delicate fragility; the idea of reclaiming Europe for the "indigenous" white (Christian) folks by forcibly excluding nonwhite people as "alien" to Europe; the calls for crusades and *Reconquista*; the recurrent waves of demographic panic; the fear of losing power, control, hegemony, majority advantage; dystopic projections of racial suicide, genocide, replacement; and the call for the white savior, the prince, the warrior, the hero.

Nothing new there. In fact, repetition is key to making these ideas convincing. By repeating the same claims, the audience may accept those claims as factual truth even if they are not, because what is said rings so familiar that it feels right. But how do you resell tired ideas with known detrimental potential? To Tarrant, this was a serious problem to consider. "While the movement itself, at least in the vanguard stage, does not need to have the support of the entire population, eventually we will need our people to join our new society, and voluntarily. They must be willing and wishing to be a part of this new future we envision."[232]

How do you make something look fresh that the general public may think has passed its expiration date? Gunning down unarmed Muslims was far from original, neither as video game nor as news – not to a generation brought up alongside the War on Terror. However, livestreaming an unfolding massacre from the position of a first-person-shooter video game really was. Adding to his innovation, Tarrant topped his performance with fascist chic and gamer culture idioms to please the tech-savvy youth he sought to bond with. By talking the talk, he wanted them to walk the walk. "Whilst we may use edgy humour and memes in the vanguard stage, and to attract a young audience, eventually we will need to show the reality of our thoughts and our more serious intents and wishes for the future."[233]

Tarrant spared no effort in making the Christchurch massacre go viral. Days in advance he had announced his intentions by tweeting photos of his weapons: two military-style semiautomatic AR-15s, shotguns, and a lever-action firearm, completely covered with fascist references and allusions to "heroes," including Italian racist serial killer Luca Traini, Canadian mosque-attendee shooter Alexandre Bisonette, Swedish school-children attacker Andon Lundin Pettersson, and Ukrainian-British anti-Muslim assassin Pavlo Lapshyn. Bringing his guns, a knife, and incendiary devices to set the mosque aflame, Tarrant dressed up in a bulletproof vest, military clothing, and a helmet, on which he mounted a strobe light to confuse his victims and a GoPro camera to livestream the bloodbath he intended to accomplish. After arriving in Christchurch and before driving down to the Al Noor Mosque, he sent a stream of emails to the government and media outlets, mailed out his *Great Replacement* manifesto, and posted an

[232] Tarrant, 2019a, p. 45. [233] Tarrant, 2019a, p. 45.

invitation to his fellow "cobbers" on the 8chan forum to watch him kill Muslim "invaders" on a Facebook livestream.[234]

Putting the gear into drive, Tarrant turned to the audience: "Remember lads, subscribe to PewDiePie," he said, in reference to Swedish YouTube entertainer/gamer Felix Kjellberg and his "diss" competition with the Indian T-Series channel for the position as the world's most-subscribed YouTuber, a non-event engaging an audience of several hundred million. Tarrant added a soundtrack to his live killing stream, loaded with references to colonial war and genocide, as noted in the Introduction. He drove toward the Al Noor Mosque to the tones of "Serbia Strong," a song from the Yugoslavian civil war lyricizing genocide on Muslims, known in the alt-right as "Remove Kebab": "The wolves are coming to fight/Be afraid/Karadžić will lead the Serbs to glory/We will burn you all down."[235] As Tarrant parked his car in the alley adjacent to the mosque and brought out his guns from the trunk, the music shifted to "The British Grenadiers," a British Empire marching song: "The townsmen cry/'Hurrah, boys, here comes a Grenadier!'/Some talk of Alexander/and some of Hercules/But of all the world' s brave heroes/there's none that can compare."

Early on Friday afternoon, Christchurch time (late morning in New York; past midnight in London), Tarrant walked up to the mosque entrance, shotgun raised. "Hello Brother," a man at the door said. Tarrant did not know the man was Haji Daoud Nabi, nor did he know the names of anyone else he killed that day. He shot Nabi at close range, and encountered Mounir Soliman, Sayeed Ali, Amjad Hamid, and Hussein Moustafa by the entrance. Soliman was a designer engineer who, like Tarrant, had moved to Christchurch from Australia; Ali was a lead developer at a tech company and a father of three; Hamid was a heart doctor and a rural hospital consultant who had served his community in this capacity for more than twenty years; and Moustafa was a retired accountant of seventy years who served his

---

[234] Tarrant, Tweet, March 13, 2019f; Tweet, March 13, 2019g; Tweet, March 13, 2019h; Tweet, March 15, 2019i; Tweet, March 15, 2019j.

[235] Tarrant, Facebook live stream, 2019b. Radovan Karadžić was president of Republika Srpska from 1992 to 1996. In 2019, he was sentenced to life imprisonment for crimes against humanity, including the 1995 genocide in Srebrenica.

congregation as a volunteer, cleaning and teaching Arabic. Tarrant did not know anything of that. To him they were matter that was out of place, brown Muslim bodies in white Euroland territory, and therefore filth he was obliged to clean away. He shot them dead and walked into the mosque, the sound of the British colonial march music now mixed up with the cries of terrified children hearing the shots and sensing danger and death.[236]

Tarrant continued into the mosque, his guns pointing forward, shooting, systematically slaying whoever he found, young and old, men and women. He came to kill at the time for Friday prayer, when he knew the mosque would be packed with locals. Having murdered his way forward, he entered the main prayer hall, where an estimated 120 people had gathered. Having heard the shooting outside, they had gathered in two groups, on each side of the hall. Tarrant fired fiercely at one group, shooting indiscriminately, changing magazines of sixty rounds and firing again, switching between the two groups of people seeking to protect each other with their soft bodies. On turning again, Tarrant was tackled from the side by Naeem Rashid, a local teacher, who tried to take his gun. Falling to his knees, Tarrant killed Rashid but saw that scores of people had managed to escape in the commotion, among them Ambreen, Rashid's wife, and two of their children, Abdullah and Ayaan. Their third child, Talha, was slayed by Tarrant, who had no idea whose child he was. He did not care about their lives; he cared about their deaths, and the message their deaths sent.

Tarrant approached the pile of bodies by one wall, looking for signs of life to end. One of them was Mucaad Ibrahim, a three-year-old who was sitting in his father Aden's lap; Tarrant shot him in the chest and then killed his father. Mucaad, covered with blood, looked dead as his father fell, but suddenly cried "Daddy, daddy." Reacting to the sound, Tarrant turned around and put a bullet in Mucaad's head, between his big, brown eyes.[237]

---

[236] Beynen, 2019; ""New Zealand's Tech Community Mourns the Loss of Two Members in the Christchurch Shooting," 2019; RNZCGP, 2020; *The Queen vs Brenton Harrison Tarrant*, 2020; Tarrant, Facebook Live stream, 2019b.

[237] Beynen, 2019; "New Zealand's Tech Community Mourns the Loss of Two Members in the Christchurch Shooting," 2019; RNZCGP, 2020; *The Queen vs Brenton Harrison Tarrant*, 2020; Tarrant, Facebook Live stream, 2019b.

Tarrant went out to his car for new guns and ammunition and returned to the mosque to kill what life remained, including young women who were bleeding on the street, crying for help. He again returned to his car and drove down to Linwood Mosque to the sound of "Fire" by Arthur Brown to continue the killing: "I am the god of hellfire/I bring you fire/I'll take you to burn/Fire/To destroy all you've done/Fire/To end all you've become/I'll feel your burn!"

Tarrant shot 107 people that day, 51 of whom died. Later, he would regret only not having been able to set the mosques aflame, and not having killed more people.[238]

Meanwhile, the anonymous viewers who followed Tarrant's Facebook livestream went from confounded to enthusiastic as they commented on the unfolding events in the online chat. "This is a larp [live-action role play] isn't it?" one of the anons (anonymous users) asked; "not larp," another anon replied, "actually happening. delete this thread now or its gonna be the end of 8pol." "Good luck shitposter. Rolling for many dead chinks and niggers." The chat continued as Tarrant arrived at the second mosque, got out of his car, entered the building, and began to kill whoever he found as he passed through the rooms. "Holy fuck," an anonymous onlooker exclaimed. "OP fucking delivered I just saw him kill so many fucking hajis." "HOLY SHIT!!!" another replied, "THE DIGITS OF GOD!"

To provide a glimpse of what was going on in the chat as spectators reacted to the live killings, I will cite a few more comments. "Someone better have fucking recorded that shit, it was fucking amazing," an anonymous user wrote several minutes into the massacre. "Seriously did no one here save any of it?" another worried. Fellow spectators assured they had in staccato prose: "I've got the word doc"; "the pdf"; "the vids of the FB stream." "He's the real deal," proclaimed another anon.

---

[238] Having emptied his magazines in the assault against people in the Linwood Mosque, Tarrant ran back to his car and drove toward Ashburton to attack a third mosque, with the guns remaining in the car. However, Tarrant was rammed by a police car en route and made no attempt to resist arrest; *The Queen vs Brenton Harrison Tarrant*, 2020; Tarrant, Facebook Live stream, 2019b.

Cheers, laughs, and celebrations mixed with voices concerned with saving and disseminating the massacre and the political manifesto it advertised. "Sounds fun," a latecomer said when he learned about the massacre he had partly missed; "back on now," a thrilled anon announced when Tarrant returned with more guns from his truck and the action began anew. "Best of luck, Brenton Tarrant," an onlooker wrote, which set off a series of similar comments. "See you in Valhalla, BT," someone replied. "Brenton Tarrant is a fucking hero," another confirmed. "Aryan genes," a third added. Anonymous chat participants found the killings they saw entertaining, gratifying, genius: "HAHAHA HE PLAYED REMOVE KEBAB EN ROUTE! I'M DYIN' OVER HERE!" "That video is so goddamn good," a spectator exclaimed. "Best start to a weekend ever," another agreed. "Mission accomplished," wrote an anon when the livestreaming was finally over. "Stream saved," another announced. "And nothing of value was lost."[239]

The livestreamed massacre quickly spread through cyberspace. Facebook blocked 1.5 million uploads within the first twenty-four hours, assuring its users that "terror attacks and the support thereof . . . violates community standards." Yet, the livestream kept circulating[240] and unleashed frantic creativity in the white fascist digital community. Anonymous white nationalists posted jokes, memes, pics, clips, edited films, video games, quizzes: "Guess the body count."

Anons railed against the "thought police" trying to "censor" the massacre, sentimentally reminding each other of Tarrant's last words before going live: "you are all top blokes and the best bunch of cobbers a man could ask for. I have provided links to my writings below, please do your part by spreading my message, making memes and shitposting as you usually do. If I don't survive the attack, goodbye, godbless and I will see you all in Valhalla!" Obviously, Tarrant's word struck a chord among 8chan's fascist users. "Make sure to repost it, it would be a shame if we lost a fellow anon's manifesto," an anon replied. "Imagine if we didn't have Breivik's writings."[241]

---

[239] Tarrant, Facebook Live stream chat, 2019c.

[240] "Update on New Zealand," 2019; Mitchell, 2019; Jhirad, 2019.

[241] Tarrant, Facebook Live stream chat continued, 2019d.

The Christchurch massacre was a hit in the fascist segment of the gamer community. The genocide video game *Jesus Strikes Back: Judgement Day* – offered for a symbolic $14.88 – was quickly updated to allow gamers to play Brant T, the Australian, and shoot homosexuals, antifa, feminists, abortionists, and nonwhites to assist JC (Jesus Christ) in the fight to save the world for white heterosexual people. Another "indie" game celebrating Christchurch was *Shitposter*, in which "B. Torrent" unleashes the "ultimate practical joke upon Clowntown. JooTube may remove his videos, but they cannot stop this hilarious practical joke from going viral."[242] Games like these come with a caveat: nothing is for real, nothing is serious. "We develop satirical parody video games for real epic gamerz," said game producers 2GenPro.[243] It is all for fun, much like earlier games such as *Ethnic Cleansing* and *Muslim Massacre* by other producers. "All of our games are satirical produce," a 2GenPro disclaimer reads. "All individuals and characters that are featured in Jesus Strikes Back: Judgement Day are purely fictional,[244] like *Mussolino, Bolselnoro, Tromp, B. Torrent* and other 'free people'."[245]

Eccentric as such games may seem, they are not that different from mainstream games where a player chooses an avatar and ventures into unknown territory, be it Iraq or Azeroth, to kill the enemy, whether Arab or Orc. From its inception in the 1930s, networking computer culture was driven by the military-industrial complex, with important connections to corporate and political interests. This was reflected in the first computer games that were not simply digitalized versions of something else: *Spacewar* (1962) and *Gran Trak, Tank, Wheels, Gun Fight*, and *Sea Wolf* (1976), in which hypermasculine white heroes drove fast machines and gunned down enemies.[246] By the twenty-first century, the gaming industry "[generated] more employment and revenue than either the professional music industry

---

[242] 2GenPro, 2019a; 2GenPro, *Jesus Strikes Back: Judgement Day*, n.d.

[243] 2GenPro, 2019b. [244] 2GenPro, 2019c.

[245] 2GenPro, *Jesus Strikes Back: Judgement Day*, n.d.

[246] *Spacewar* was preceded by games imitating non-digital games, such as *Tic tac toe* (1950), *Nim* (1951), and *Pong* (first version 1954; second arcade version 1970).

or the Hollywood film industry," which makes video games not only profitable but highly influential culturally and politically.[247]

Christchurch blurred the distinction between trolling and terrorism, Julia Ebner observes,[248] and was a deadly illustration of the potential real-life impact of online activism. The communication space of the Internet has long been home to people in the radical nationalist landscape, in use not only as a tool but as a constitutive part of existence. It is here that a significant portion of the self-appointed white resistance have their incubators, meeting grounds, love affairs, conflicts, campaigns, and battles, and it is also the place where many of them work and spend much of their time. Cyberspace is where they market things and themselves, listen to music, play games, go shopping, get rich, get robbed, get fooled, become successful, or fail; it is a place of learning and experience, where they are educated and bring other people up, get them "red-pilled," "white-pilled," "black-pilled," as the sequential fascist references to *The Matrix* go.

Travelers in the radical nationalist landscape were early users of the Internet. Historically, the first instance of networked computers was established in National Socialist Germany as far back as 1933, for military purposes.[249] In 1984, years before the inventions of the World Wide Web and the HTTP and HTML standards, Louis Beam organized the Aryan Nations Liberty Board linking together a dozen computerized white nationalist information bases, which was the first civilian computerized network operated by fascists. The first US presidential candidate to launch a website was Bob Dole, who ran against Bill Clinton in 1996. Don Black, former Imperial Wizard of the Knights of the Ku Klux Klan, had launched the Stormfront website one year earlier, in March 1995. More than twenty-five years later, Stormfront remains an important platform, while Dole is forgotten. White nationalists are still at the cutting edge of digital communication technologies, with their "Alt-Tech" and Dark Net efforts to evade

---

[247] Bezio, 2018. [248] Ebner, 2020, p. 237.

[249] After the war, several of these German experts in computer technology were brought to the USA through Operation Paperclip, which contributed to the USA becoming an important home for technological innovations in the field.

the enhanced possibilities of surveillance that come with the new technologies.

A couple of decades into the 2000s, "there is no longer a simple distinction between online and offline campaigning practices" as they are interconnected, intertwined, inter-responsive, and inter-affecting. Contemporary radical nationalist politics are increasingly "postdigital," argue Stephen Albrecht, Maik Fielitz, and Nick Thurston, using the concept to analyze the "shocking power" of radical nationalists "to mobilize online and offline in terms of this pervasive inter-effectivity."[250]

In the digital communities where gaming culture intersects with alt-right online culture and the tech-savvy breeds of white fascist youth culture, Tarrant was great news. "Master Chief Brenton Harrison Tarrant卐, a.k.a. the Kiwi Kebab Killer, is a heroic IRL JC Denton Aussie troll who took it upon himself to remove the Mooslem filth," wrote Encyclopedia Dramatica. "Before going on his rampage, Brenton posted his manifesto to 8chan and 4chan; there, he namedropped famous Swedish neon-nazi PewDiePie and Norwegian WoW aficionado Anders Behring Breivik as inspirations. This resulted in massive amounts of lulz and butthurt from the lamestream media who took his massive shitpost of a manifesto at face value, including the ever-trustworthy (((CNN)))."[251]

On August 13, 2019, Tarrant suddenly made a hero's comeback on 4chan, with a letter that had somehow got through security and was posted online. It was published on August 13, 2019, but was dated 4 July in allusion to Breivik's Declaration of European Independence.[252] Tarrant's sudden reappearance in 4chan's digital fascist community was sensational. The

---

[250] *Post-digital* refers to a state in which the disruption of the webolution has already happened, and refers to a condition "constituted by the naturalization of pervasive and connected computing processes and outcomes in everyday life, such that digitality is now inextricable from the way we live while its forms, functions and effects are no longer necessarily perceptible" (Albrecht et al., 2019, p. 10).

[251] Encyclopedia Dramatica. The enclosing of a term in triple-parentheses marks it as something or someone Jewish.

[252] Tarrant, "Hello Alan," Letter to 4chan, 2019e.

letter is styled as an answer to a (real or faked) Russian admirer and includes references to the fascist romance with Russia as the Great White Bastion and the Russian occult-metal rapper Dirty Ramirez's "Toxin" video. While Ramirez's Russian lyrics were lost on many of Tarrant's admirers, the YouTube video immediately gained hundreds of thousands views. "It's FM Christchurch," a commenter solemnly stated. "Blessed by Saint BT himself," confirmed another anon. "No idea what he's saying but this song is insanely good," an anon wrote. "Better play it in a Subaru Outback," an anon said, with reference to the car Tarrant drove during his livestream.[253]

Tarrant informs his followers about his political views with reference to Plato's *Republic*, Richard Dawkin's theory of memetics, Carl Gustaf Jung's views on inherited racial conscious and subconscious, i.e., the connection between the organic race and its racial soul, and his belief in the hierarchical nature of nature. As an influence, Tarrant points to Sir Oswald Mosley, the eloquent British fascist orator.

Casually, Tarrant provides a glimpse into everyday prison life. It's not too bad; he does not do much but talk to his lawyers and prepare for his trial. He cannot go into detail on feelings and regrets, but assures his readers that he has "no concern" for himself and only worries "for Europe's future." Tarrant urges his readers to prepare, as "there is a great conflict on the horizon" that will bring a "great amount of bloodshed."[254]

In *The Selfish Gene* (1976), Dawkins coined the term "meme," which he sees as a "unit of culture" – an idea, a conviction, a behavior, a pattern – "hosted" in the mind of an individual, which then may be reproduced and transmitted by jumping from one mind to another – exactly what Tarrant hoped to achieve by getting readers "out there" to replicate his action. "Lets get this party started lads," a 4channer commented on the Dirty Ramirez "Toxin" video. "The kind of music heroes listen to," another said. "I could Go Pro to this."[255]

---

[253] Dirty Ramirez, 2018, comments 2019/2020; Dirty Ramirez, "Toxic," lyrics, 2018.

[254] Tarrant, "Hello Alan," Letter to 4chan, 2019e.

[255] Dirty Ramirez, 2018, comments 2019/2020.

The Game to End It All

Tarrant's anti-Muslim massacre represents an accelerationist fascist effort to gamify mass murder. *The Great Replacement* is loaded with references to digital culture, connecting gamer culture, fan culture, the deep right, and fascism, and seeking to get readers to think that it is a matter of distinguishing between those who get it and those who do not. The manifesto features ironic, low-quality trolling, such as Tarrant pretending to having been radicalized by *Spyro the Dragon* and *Fortnite* and illuminated by the wisdom of Candance Owens.[256] He nods at fandome memes (Navy Seals Copypasta) and refers to gaming culture (PewDiePie; "Gas Gas Gas" in *Initial D*, a game adapted on the street racing manga series by Shuichi Shigeno); he was rewarded by himself becoming a meme circulating in alt-right forums, even appearing as a GIF on the websites of the *Daily Mail* and *The Sun*, made from a clip of Tarrant's livestream showing the gun going into the mosque and shooting, construing killing Muslims as entertainment.[257]

According to Andrew Anglin, founding editor of the unapologetically fascist *Daily Stormer* (named after the lowbrow anti-Semitic German tabloid *Der Stürmer*) who wrote the *Normies Guide to the Alt-Right*, the tone should be light if you want to get a racist message across. "Idealism must be couched in irony in order to be taken seriously." People should not know if we are joking or not. GTKRWN – Gas the Kikes, Race War Now. Joke about the Holocaust. Laugh at mass murder; laugh at people who get offended; laugh at those stupid enough to think that we really want to gas kikes. Only, we do.[258]

The use of irony, satire, laughs, and subcultural idioms enables fascists to hide in plain sight. Doublespeak, what Graham Macklin describes as a frontstage-backstage dynamic of "ideological bifurcation," has long been a feature of fascist communication.[259] Online anon fascists take turns in promoting fascist lone wolves, making each new killer a hero, an icon, a meme, a GIF, a laugh. Photoshop the head of Luca Traini, the Italian lone

---

[256] Tarrant, 2019a, p. 17.

[257] Tarrant, Facebook Live stream, 2019b; Lorenz, 2019; Evans, 2019; Know Your Meme Internet Database, n.d.; Ebner, 2020.

[258] Anglin, 2016. [259] Macklin, 2014; May & Feldman, 2019; Greene, 2019.

wolf who shot African migrants in Macerat, onto the cover of the video game *God of War* and rename it *God of Race War* and add a Black Sun in the back; celebrate Breivik as *Breivhart*; make a Dylann Roof meme with the caption "IF YOUR SCARED TO GO TO CHURCH"; photoshop Swedish lone wolf killer Anton Lundin Pettersson into a sword-slinging Pepe the Frog. Does anyone get upset? You are just trolling, joking around. Then, sit back and wait for next lone wolf to do his part in pushing the race war closer to fruition.

As observed by Marc Tuters, the "meme also draws its transgressive appeal from its *subjunctive adjacency* to actual violence – violence made possible thanks to the deepvernacular web's digital dualism." Turning Tarrant into pop memes, such as the Kebab Shooter or "Who Wants to be a Killionaire?" becomes fascist fun by portraying reality as wished-for reality that yet is reality, making it only a joke – except that it is not. Thus, online fascist subjunctive celebration of weaponized whiteness reflects and impacts offline reality, as demonstrated by the sequential materialization of lone wolf killers entering schools, mosques, synagogues, churches, plazas, and markets.

On April 29, 2019, John T. Earnest opened fire in a synagogue in Poway in San Diego County, California, killing one and injuring three, including the rabbi. Before his assault, he thanked the 8chan "shitposters" and posted a manifesto claiming to have been inspired by Tarrant. "Keep up the memes of Brenton Tarrant," Earnest wrote. "Tarrant was a catalyst for me personally. He showed me that it could be done. And that it needed to be done": "I'd rather die in glory or spend the rest of my life in prison than waste away knowing that I did nothing to stop this evil."[260]

"In general, I support the Christchurch shooter and his manifesto," above-mentioned Patrick Crusius wrote before entering the Walmart in El Paso, Texas to shoot "Hispanic invaders." Crusius also credited Tarrant, saying he made up his mind and chose his target after having read *The Great Replacement*. "INACTION IS A CHOICE," Tarrant exclaimed. Crusius agreed, announcing he would do his part. "I am honored to head the fight to reclaim my country from destruction."[261]

---

[260] Earnest, 2019. Posted at 8chan and reposted at Daily Buzz. [261] Crusius, 2019.

The following week, on August 10, 2019, Philip Manshaus, a white Norwegian son of a billionaire, put a video camera on his helmet but failed to get the stream uploaded online. He posted a meme referring to Crusius and Earnest as Saint Tarrant's disciples, and claimed to have been "elected" by Tarrant to commit a Muslim massacre at the Al-Noor Islamic Center on the outskirts of Oslo. Having killed his stepsister, he dressed up in military clothing with *Totenkopf* insignia, covered his face with a skull mask, and filmed himself driving down to the nearby mosque to "kill as many Muslims as possible." He drew his guns and stormed the mosque but was overpowered by retired Pakistani Air Force officer Mohammad Rafiq, who was in the mosque preparing for the Eid al-Adha celebrations.[262]

At the Endchan platform, Manshaus left his last message: "well cobbers it's my time, i was elected by saint tarrant after all. we can't let this go on, you gotta bump the race war thread irl and if you're reading this you have been elected by me."[263]

7 Hero Quest

Fascism offers its adherents to be part of something greater than themselves, invoking their desire for heroism, glory, and honor, and inducing their capacities for self-sacrifice, discipline, and violence. Centered on its core myth of national rebirth and the becoming of the New Man, fascism appeals to the Faustian task of metamorphosis, of individual, national, and racial grandeurization, heroification, deification.

Across the political landscape of radical nationalism there are recurrent references to Nietzsche's *Übermensch* and Jung's archetype of the hero, he who springs from the depths of the collective unconscious of the Aryan race's soul and embarks on an adventurous journey, confronts the dragon, the monster of darkness, and returns a new man.

This hero quest, I suggest, lies at the heart of the lone wolf attraction among white radical nationalists. To them, he is not a lone-acting terrorist, a creature of the shadows, a sneaky coward who attacks soft civilian targets, women, children, the elderly, and noncombatants; rather, he is a mythic

[262] Bangstad. 2020. [263] Manshaus, 2019.

lone wolf hero recognizable from the sagas, the Hollywood epics, the Marvel comics. He is the masked Superhero, the lone avenger, the outlaw in service of a higher law, the Superman. To be a real man, you need a mission and a woman to save. "A true white man fights," David Lane emphasized, "because the beauty of the white Aryan woman must not perish from the earth."[264]

Most white men of today have been exposed to supermen from a young age, through narratives, comics, movies, TV series, artwork, and video games that to many a young mind contributed to forming dreams of becoming a hero, overcoming individual weaknesses, standing up to the bullies, defeating the enemies, surmounting the obstacles, crushing the monster, gaining the admiration of others, stunning the world, and winning the hearts of their loved ones.

The Superman genre is a representation of male fantasies, linked with the ancient sagas and rearticulated through popular mass culture, reenacted through stories from Hercules to Batman. Essential to constructions of masculinity in the everyday making of men in Western and global culture, the superhero fed into the fascist projects of the early twentieth and twenty-first centuries as evidenced by fascist cults of male virilities, the elevation of hypermasculine bodies in fascist art, sculpture, pulp, propaganda, memes, video games, and literature, the role of gymnastics, sports, outback trekking, and body work in the fascist project, and its Faustian quest to make men out of boys and gods out of men.[265] It is a discernible aspect of the appeal of the lone wolf, too.

According to the rules of the lone wolf, a man who wishes to join the leaderless armed resistance should go underground by melting into the general population. He should not flag with his identity, should take no credit, and should tell no one. In everyday life, he should adopt a grey, anonymous, everyday identity, abstaining from attracting attention through his looks, ways, words, and behavior. He might be a wolf, but he should look like a poodle. He should hide his true self, his inner heroic being, and pass like Clark Kent from Smallville, Kansas: a timid, nearsighted, and uncertain man working as an insignificant reporter at a daily in the

[264] Lane, Interview, November 12, 1996. [265] Spackman, 1996; Mangan, 1999.

metropolis only to be close to his secret love, Lois Lane, the acclaimed star journalist of stunning beauty, who (initially) only has eyes for the Superman. When the supervillain enters and threatens the good and inno-cent people of the city, country, and world, Clark Kent dashes into the closet, store room, phone booth, alley, or bathroom to change into the Superman and flies over the heads of the awestruck folks to confront evil as it comes. He defeats the supervillain and wins the admiration of his love. Dreaming of changing into a lone wolf to save the beauty of the white woman, the race, and the future for white children is not all that different.

The fascist dimension of the superhero mythos has not been lost on the fascists themselves. A number of prominent American radical nationalist writers of different shades have contributed their analyses of Batman, Superman, and other superheroes in the Counter-Currents anthology *Dark Right: Batman Viewed from the Right*. "Globalism necessarily requires the eradication of all organic cultures, traditions, and identities," editors Greg Johnson and Gregory Hood state in the introduction. Yet, "even the most atomized individual desires some kind of mythos, some image of the transcendent and that which is above." In a time of materialism and spiritual emptiness, "where culture has been replaced by consumerism, where 'God is dead' and reality is experienced on a screen, the closest glimpse most people have on the sublime is a superhero." The "entire superhero genre is inherently antiliberal," Jonson and Hood argue – none more so than Batman, not least as rebooted in Frank Miller's *The Dark Knight Returns* and Christopher Nolan's Dark Knight trilogy, where the character "is not just antiliberal, but decidedly Right-wing," that is, fascist.[266]

Not every superhero character is met with fascist approval. Greg Jonson points out that the genre in comics and movies was largely a creation of Jewish cultural producers and superheroes may function as "symbolic proxies for Jews," immensely powerful aliens and freaks who form their own secret societies operating above the law, as evidenced by the Justice League, the Avengers, and the X-Men, which are all "committed to the morality of egalitarian humanism and benevolently serving the interest of humanity."[267] Perhaps no character is as problematic to fascist reviewers as

[266] Johnson & Hood, 2018. [267] Johnson, 2018, p. 83f.

Superman himself. "I have never liked the character of the Superman," confided Trevor Lynch, author of *White Nationalist Guide to the Movies*. "He is simply an alien, who looks like us and comes equipped with superpowers. From a Nietzschean or Faustian standpoint that translates to no appeal."[268]

Gregory Hood (aka James Kirkpatrick, aka Kevin DeAnna) finds Superman more ambivalent as a character. On the one hand, he is the all-American white-hat good boy who stands for truth, justice, and the American way; he is a creation of Jews and a foe of the Nazis, who acts like a big blue boy scout, that is, a manifestation of the inherently antiwhite System he is constantly called upon to save. Yet, on the other hand, Superman is raised in small-town Middle America by patriotic, plain-speaking, clean-living, churchgoing, Methodist, authentic white American rural folks. Superman is an alien, definitely, but from a superior white Aryan planet – there are no nonwhite Kryptonians – organized hierarchically along caste lines, and planted and nurtured among white folks on white land, thus personifying a dual white heritage: the white world of Odal farmers and tradition and the white world of innovation, expansion, and space age advancement.

In the opening scenes of *Man of Steel* (2013), Hood points out, the young Clark Kent is seen reading Plato's *Republic* and democracy is portrayed as incapable of defending itself and its constituency when the supervillain General Zod (ZOG?) appears to implement the Great Replacement by pushing out the native white people to make the planet safe for colonization by aliens. It takes extralegal violence to stop Zod's evil scheme. Hood acknowledges that the Man of Steel is not deeply anti-Zionist, but appreciates the effort of Zack Snyder and David Goyer to construe Superman as a white Christ, an Aryan warrior god, arising from the soil of Kansas to meet the challenge and defend the good and decent native folk from the evil cabal planning their replacement.[269]

If Superman generally remains problematic to white fascists as too pro-System, anti-Nazi, and anti-traditionalist, Batman is another story. While Superman is almost invulnerable, and therefore hardly a hero, Trevor

[268] Lynch, 2018; 2013.   [269] Hood, 2018.

Lynch reasons, Batman "is a true Nietzschean Superman." Batman is a man who made himself more than a man, a Superman, pointing to the fascist vision of white Aryan men reaching into divinity.[270] Zachary O. Ray of Identity Evrupa, an Americanized version of Generation Identity that claims to fight for a white world that is "both traditional and Faustian,"[271] agrees. *The Dark Knight Returns*, he claims, portrays an alt-right hero's journey, as it "chronicles Western man's spiritual struggle toward superhuman reawakening against modern egalitarian mediocrity."[272] Of course, the "most rightwing aspect of Batman is his fascist use of force" and his recognition of the fact that "order must be brought about by violence."[273]

To Jason Reza Jorjani, an Iranian-American fascist intellectual and editor of Arktos Media and co-founder of AltRight Corporation and AltRight.com before his falling out with Richard Spencer, Batman is not an Apollonian emissary of truth, justice, and the American way, but comes from a world of shadow and darkness as the native son of Gotham, the archetypal New York, the modern Rome or Babylon – the most corrupt, materialist, rotten city-state on earth. He was not endowed from birth with superpowers; his extraordinary abilities are born of long, hard training and lethal confrontation with his enemies. Fighting a series of villains produced by the multilayered globalist world order, Batman is recurrently pitted against the officers of law and order, which highlights the epos' inherent critique of the current political order. The Dark Knight trilogy, Jorjani argues, explores why democracy is a misguided political system that first must be exempted during the state of exception called to meet the challenge of the series of supervillains from the League of Shadows, and must then be permanently suspended under a Caesarian dark enlightenment regime modeled on Plato's *Republic*, hailed by Jornani as the most antidemocratic text in the history of philosophy, with Batman serving as a dark Guardian.[274]

In *The Dark Knight* (2008), Christopher Nolan puts Batman the vigilante into the role of the Roman dictator. "When their enemies were at the gates,

---

[270] Lynch, 2018, p. 141.

[271] Quote by Guillaume Faye, used by Identity Evropa, "Action Report," n.d.

[272] Ray, 2018, p. 151. [273] Windsor, 2018, p. 107. [274] Jorjani, 2018.

the Romans would suspend democracy and appoint one man to protect the city. It wasn't considered an honor; it was considered a public duty." Wayne, reborn as Batman, may hesitate at performing the function of the sovereign, but ultimately transgresses the law in order to restore it. This poses a question to the audience, Jonson and Hood argue.[275] If the system is so inherently corrupt that it can only be saved by violating it, why then should extraordinary men sacrifice themselves to save it? Maybe the rotten system cannot be saved, but needs to be destroyed and reborn?

That is the conclusion of the lone wolf.

[275] Johnson & Hood, 2018.

References

Interviews by the author

John Baumgardner, MacIntosh, Florida, November 1, 1996.

Tom Brady (pseudonym), Wisconsin, August 19, 1998.

Anders Behring Breivik, Telemark fengsel, Skien, June 19, 2014.

Randy Duey, Mandelville, Louisiana, May 20, 1997.

George Hawthorne, Windsor, Ontario, Canada, October 2, 1996.

Richard Kemp, Sheridan, Oregon, May 8, 1997.

David Lane, Florence, Colorado, November 12, 1996.

Peter Mangs, Saltvik Prison, Härnösand, November 10, 2013.

Peter Mangs, Saltvik Prison, Härnösand, November 11, 2013.

Peter Mangs, Saltvik Prison, Härnösand, December 7, 2013.

Peter Mangs, Saltvik Prison, Härnösand, December 8, 2013.

Peter Mangs, Saltvik Prison, Härnösand, December 13, 2013.

Peter Mangs, Saltvik Prison, Härnösand, January 10, 2014.

Peter Mangs, Saltvik Prison, Härnösand, January 11, 2014.

Peter Mangs, Saltvik Prison, Härnösand, June 16, 2014.

Peter Mangs, Saltvik Prison, Härnösand, June 17, 2014.

Peter Mangs, Saltvik Prison, Härnösand, April 29, 2015.

Peter Mangs, Saltvik Prison, Härnösand, April 30, 2015.

Rudolf Mangs, Boca Raton, Florida, February 1, 2015.

Rudolf Mangs, Boca Raton, Florida, February 2, 2015.

Rudolf Mangs, Boca Raton, Florida, February 3, 2015.

Rudolf Mangs, Boca Raton, Florida, February 4, 2015.

Rudolf Mangs, Boca Raton, Florida, February 5, 2015.

Tom Metzger, Carlsbad, California, December 16, 1996.

Tom Metzger, Fallbrook, California, December 15, 1998.

David Tate, Potosi, Mineral Point, Missouri, May 22, 1997.

Gary Yabrough, Leavenworth, Kansas, April 15, 1997.

Lone Wolf Declarations, Manifestos

Breivik, Anders Behring, *2083: A European Declaration of Independence*, Self-published, July 22, 2011.

Crusius, Patrick, *The Inconvenient Truth*, self-published, August 3, 2019.

Earnest, John, "An Open Letter" [*John Earnest Manifesto*], self-published, April 28, 2019.

Lane, David, *White Genocide Manifesto*, self-published, 1988 [republished 1994 by 14 Word Press].

Mangs, Peter *German Philosophy*, manuscript, n.d.

McVeigh, Timothy, "An Essay of Hypocrisy," letter, March 1998.

McVeigh, Timothy, "I Explain Herein Why I Bombed the Murrah Federal Building in Oklahoma City," Fox News, April 26, 2001.

Pettersson, Anton Lundin, *Avskedsbrev*. Dnr 5000-K1353421-15, 2015.

Tarrant, Brenton, *The Great Replacement*, self-published, 2019a.

The Army of God Manual, n.d.

Documents, Unpublished Sources

2GenPro, "Disclaimer," www.2gen.pro/disclaimer/, 2019a.

2GenPro, *Shitposter*, www.2gen.pro/the-shitposter/ 2019b.

2GenPro, "Statement," www.2gen.pro/about-us, 2019c.

2GenPro, *Jesus Strikes Back: Judgement Day*, www.2gen.pro/2020/05/27/jesus-strikes-back-judgment-day-remastered/n.d.

An Act To regulate the Immigration of Aliens into the United States, Section 39, 1903. FIFTY-SEVENTH CONGRESS.SFSS. II.CHs.1012,1013. 1903, sfss II. CHs, 1012, 1013, 1903.

Anmälan, P.M., Beslag; Avlidne Ahmed Hassan; Avlidne Lavin Eskander Avlidne Nazir Azmo; Wahid Kosa Mohammad; David Issa; Dnr. 5000-K1353421-15, 2015.

Breivik, Anders Behring, Testimony in court, trial date April 17; April 20, 2012. Oslo Tingrett, TOSLO-2011–118627-24, 2012.

Breivik, Anders Behring, Letter to author, April 2, 2013.

Breivik, Anders Behring, Letter to author, February 21, 2014.

Breivik, Anders Behring, Letter to author, October 20, 2015.

Breivik, Anders Behring, Letter to author, August 5, 2016.

Breivik, Anders Behring, Letter to author, June 17, 2018.

Dirty Ramirez, "Toxin," Максим Иванов, YouTube, www.youtube.com /watch?v=Gdi3ZSn86kw, 2018 (original); comments 2019/2020.

Dirty Ramirez, Lyrics, Грязный Рамирес –Токсин, https://text-lyrics.ru/gl/dirty-ramires/8248-gryaznij-ramires-toksin-text-pesni.html, 2018.

"Discussion," Anton Lundin Pettersson, YouTube, www.youtube.com /user/HiphopDestroyer666/discussion.

Ekeroth, Kent, "Tal i Trelleborg," mp4, October 17, 2015.

Encyclopedia Dramatica, "Brenton Tarrant," https://encyclopediadrama tica.wiki/index.php/Brenton_Tarrant, n.d.

"FBI Director on Threat of ISIS, Cybercrime," CBS *60 Minutes*, October 5, 2014.

FBI, *Project Megiddo*, Federal Bureau of Investigation, Department of Justice, 1999.

Förhör, Beställning av hjälm och svärd på internet, Dnr 5000-K1353421-15, 2015.

Förhör med vittnen, 2010–12-02; 2011–01-11, Dnr 1200-K163215-09, 2011.

Förundersökningsprotokoll, Åklnr AM-144882–15; Polisregion Väst, Grova brott 1 PO Fyrbodal, Dnr 5000-K1353421-15, 2015.

Förundersökningsprotokoll, AM-144882–15; Anmälan, PM, Beslag; Avlidne Ahmed Hassan; Avlidne Lavin Eskander Avlidne Nazir Azmo; (skadade) Wahid Kosa Mohammad; David Issa; 5000-K1353421 -15, 2015.

Förundersökningsprotokoll, "Sms-konversation Andreas – T Diete", 2016–03-10 14:49 diarienr: 5000-K63413-16, 2016.

GMs mobil; GMs andra mobil; GMs USB, GMs stationära dator: Undersökningsprotokoll, Brottsplatsundersökning, 2016–03-31, Dnr 5000-K1353421-15, 2016.

Global Terrorism Database, "Defining Terrorism," www.start.umd.edu/gtd/, n.d.

Identity Evropa, "Action Report," www.identityevropa.com/action-report/, n.d.

Jhirad, Rahel, @RahelJhirad (2019), "Svar till @fbnewsroom," March 17, https://twitter.com/RahelJhirad; https://twitter.com/fbnewsroom/status/1107117981358682112, 2019.

Johnson, Greg & John Morgan, "The Great Replacement," *Counter-Currents Radio Podcast*, July 12, 2019.

Know Your Meme Internet Database, https://knowyourmeme.com, n.d.

Löfven, Stefan, "Tal av Stefan Löfven vid manifestationen för flyktingar," Medborgarplatsen, Stockholm, September 6, 2015.

Manshaus, Philip, Communication, Endchan, August 10, 2019.

McCulloch, Richard, *The Racial Compact: A Call for Racial Rights, Preservation, and Independence*, www.racialcompact.com/, n.d.

Oslo tingrett – Dom. 22. juli-saken. Oslo tingrett TOSLO–2011–118627–24, 24.08.2012, 2012.

Oslo Borgarting Lagmanssrett, DOM, Saksnr: 16-111749ASD-BORG/02, 01.03.2017, 2017.

"Pensionsbroms eller invandringsbroms," SD Valfilm, 2010.

Sverigedemokraterna, Presskonferens, October 15, 2015.

Tarrant, Brenton, Facebook Live stream, massacre, Christchurch, New Zealand, March 15, www.facebook.com/brenton.tarrant.9/videos/2350426065176752/, 2019b.

Tarrant, Brenton, Facebook Live stream chat, anonymous participants, March 15, https://archive.vn/dhmg8#selection-1919.1-1953.10, 2019c.

Tarrant, Brenton, Facebook Live stream chat continued, anonymous participants, March 15, https://archive.vn/dhmg8#selection-15845.0-15869.8, 2019d.

Tarrant, Brenton, "Hello Alan," Letter to 4chan, August 13 [dated July 4], https://boards.4chan.org/pol/thread/222869459, https://archive.4plebs.org/pol/thread/222869459/, 2019e.

Tarrant, Brenton, Tweet, March 13, https://twitter.com/BrentonTarrant/status/1105657000803758086, 2019f.

Tarrant, Brenton, Tweet, March 13, https://twitter.com/BrentonTarrant/status/1105657985324539907, 2019g.

Tarrant, Brenton, Tweet, March 13, https://twitter.com/BrentonTarrant/status/1105658234738626560, 2019h.

Tarrant, Brenton, Tweet, March 15, https://twitter.com/BrentonTarrant/status/1105657559938011136, 2019i.

Tarrant, Brenton, Tweet, March 15, https://twitter.com/BrentonTarrant/status/1106350936241246209, 2019j.

The Covenant, the Sword, the Arm of the Lord, File 100-HQ-487200, Federal Bureau of Investigation, 1982.

The Queen vs Brenton Harrison Tarrant, High Court of New Zealand, CRI-2019-009-2468 [2020] NZHC 2192, Judgement, August 27, 2020.

US Government Accountability Office, *Countering Violent Extremism: Actions Needed to Define Strategy and Assess Progress of Federal Efforts* (GAO-17-300), 2017.

"Update on New Zealand," Facebook Newsroom, March 18, https://newsroom.fb.com/news/2019/03/update-on-new-zealand, 2019.

Uppgifter som ej ingår i FU-protokoll. Utredningsuppgifter och anteckningar, AM-144882-15; Dnr 5000-K1353421-15, 2015; 2016.

Åkesson, Jimmie, *Sommartal*, Sölvesborg, August 2, 2014.

Printed Publications

"A Message from East Africa," *Rumiyyah*, no 2, Muharram 1438, 2016.

Agamben, Giorgio, *Homo Sacer: Sovereign Power and Bare Life*, Stanford University, 1998.

Albrecht, Stephen, Maik Fielitz, & Nick Thurston, *Post-Digital Cultures of the Far Right*, transcript Verlag, 2019.

Anglin, Andrew, "A Normie's Guide to the Alt-Right," *Daily Stormer*, August 31, 2016.

al-Awlaki, Anwar, "Shaykh Anwar's Message to the American People and Muslims in the West," *Inspire*, no. 1, Summer 1431, 2010.

Andersen, Benedict, *Imagined Communities*, rev. ed., Verso, 1991.

Andersson, Roger, Åsa Bråmå, & Jon Hogdal, *Fattiga och rika – segregerad stad*, Göteborgs stad, 2009.

Atomwaffen Division, https://atomwaffendivision.org/who-we-are/,n.d.

Ayton, Mel, *Dark Soul of the South*, Potomac Books, 2011.

Bakker, Edwin & Jeanine de Roy van Zuijdewijn (eds), *Lone-Actor Terrorism Definitional Workshop*, Royal United Services Institute for Defence and Security Studies, Countering Lone-Actor Terrorism Series, 2014.

Balaicius, Robert Alan, *The War Between the Children of Light and the Powers of Darkness*, Sacred Truth Ministries, 1997.

Bangstad, Sindre, "The 2019 Mosque Attack and Freedom of Speech in Norway," Al Jazeera, May 26, 2020.

Baranowski, Shelley & Armin Nolzen, *A Companion to Nazi Germany*, Wiley-Blackwell, 2018.

Barkun, Michael, *Religion and the Racist Right: The Origins of the Christian Identity Movement*, University of North Carolina Press, 1995.

Barkun, Michael, "Conspiracy Theory and Stigmatized Knowledge: The Basis for a New Age Racism?" *Nation and Race: The Developing Euro-*

American Racist Subculture, Jeffrey Kaplan & Tore Bjørgå (eds), Northwestern University Press, 1998.

Barkun, Michael, *A Culture of Conspiracy*, University of California Press, 2006.

Bar-On, Tamir, "The Ambiguities of the Nouvelle Droite, 1968–1999," *European Legacy*, 6:3, 2001.

Bar-On, Tamir, "The French New Right: Neither Right, Nor Left?," *Journal for the Study of Radicalism*, 8:1, 2014.

Bates, Rodger A., "Dancing With Wolves: Today's Lone Wolf Terrorists," *Journal of Public and Professional Sociology*, 4:1, 2012.

Beam, Louis, "Leaderless Resistance," *Inter-Klan Newsletter & Survival Alert*, Robert Miles, Louis Beam, & Paul Scheppf (eds), 1983.

Beam, Louis, "Leaderless Resistance," *The Seditionist*, no. 12, 1992.

Beam, Louis, "Leaderless Resistance," published by the Army of God, www.armyofgod.com/LeaderlessResistance.html,n.d.

Bennet, David, *The Party of Fear*, Vintage Books, 1995.

Bezio, Kristin M.S., "Ctrl-Alt-Del: GamerGate as a Precursor to the Rise of the Alt-Right," *Leadership*, 14:5, 2018.

Beynen, Martin van, "The Human Story behind the Victims of Christchurch's Terror Attack," Stuff, March 19, 2019.

Biehl, Janet & Peter Staudenmaier, *Ecofascism: Lessons from the German Experience*, New Compass Press, 2011.

Bjørgo, Tore & Miroslav Mareš (eds), *Vigilantism against Migrants and Minorities*, Routledge, 2019.

Bramwell, Anna, *Blood and Soil: Walther Darre and Hitler's Green Party*, Kensal Press, 1985.

BRÅ, *Brottslighet och trygghet i storstäder kartlagd*, 2012.

BRÅ, *Lethal Violence in Sweden 1990–2014*, 24, 2015.

Burgdörfer, Friedrich, *Sterben die weißen Völker*, Callwey, 1934.

Cagle, Susie, "Bees, Not Refugees," *The Guardian*, August 16, 2019.

Camus, Renaud, *Le grand remplacement*, David Reinharc, 2012.

Charlton, Lauretta, "What is the Great Replacement?" *The New York Times*, August 6, 2019.

Chatterton Williams, Thomas, "The French Origins of 'You Will Not Replace Us'," *The New Yorker*, November 27, 2017.

Corcoran, James, *Bitter Harvest: Gordon Kahl and the Rise of the Posse Comitatus in the Heartland*, Penguin, 1990.

"Detta har hänt: Flera attacker på kort tid," *SVT*, December 16, 2015.

Douglas, Mary, *Purity and Danger*, Routledge, 1966.

Ebner, Julia, *Going Dark: The Secret Social Lives of Extremists*, Bloomsbury, 2020.

Ellis, Clare, Raffaello Pantucci, Jeanine de Roy van Zuijdewijn, Edwin Bakker, Melanie Smith, Benoît Gomis, & Simon Palombi, "Analysing the Processes of Lone-Actor Terrorism: Research Findings," *Perspectives on Terrorism*, 10:2, 2016a.

Ellis, Clare, Raffaello Pantucci, Jeanine de Roy van Zuijdewijn, Edwin Bakker, Melanie Smith, Benoît Gomis, & Simon Palombi, *Lone-Actor Terrorism: Analysis Paper*, Countering Lone-Actor Terrorism Series, no. 4, 2016b.

Evans, Robert, "Shitposting, Inspirational Terrorism, and the Christchurch Mosque Massacre," *The Belling Cat*, March 15, 2019.

Faye, Guillaume, *Why We Fight: Manifesto of the European Resistance*, Arktos, 2011.

Faye, Guillaume, *The Colonisation of Europe*, Arktos, 2016.

Faye, Guillaume, *Ethnic Apocalypse*, Arktos, 2019.

Flynn, Kevin & Gary Gerhardt, *The Silent Brotherhood*, Free Press, 1999.

Fritz, Stephen , *The First Soldier: Hitler as Military Leader*, Yale University Press, 2018.

Forchtner, Bernhard (ed.), *The Far Right and the Environment*, Routledge, 2019.

Gardell, Mattias, *Rasrisk*, Federativs, 1998a.

Gardell, Mattias, "The Smorgasbord of the White Racist Counter Culture in Contemporary United States," *Racism, Ideology and Political Organization*, Charles Westin (ed.), Stockholm University: CEIFO, 1998b.

Gardell, Mattias, *Gods of the Blood: White Separatism and the Pagan Revival*, Duke University Press, 2003.

Gardell, Mattias, "White Racist Religions in the United States : From Christian Identity to Wolf Age Pagans," *Controversial New Religions*, James R. Lewis & Jesper Aagaard Petersen (eds), Oxford University Press, 2004.

Gardell, Mattias, "Crusader Dreams: Oslo 22/7, Islamophobia, and the Quest for a Monocultural Europe," *Terrorism and Political Violence*, 26:1, 2014.

Gardell, Mattias, *Raskrigaren*, Leopard, 2015a.

Gardell, Mattias, "What's Love Got to Do with It? Ultranationalism, Islamophobia, and Hate Crime in Sweden," *Journal of Religion and Violence*, 3:1, 2015b.

Gardell, Mattias, *Moskéers och Muslimska församlingars utsatthet och säkerhet i Sverige 2018*, Uppsala University: CEMFOR, 2018a.

Gardell, Mattias, "Urban Terror: The Case of Lone Wolf Peter Mangs," *Terrorism and Political Violence*, 30:5, 2018b.

Gardell, Mattias, "Pop-Up Vigilantism and Fascist Patrols in Sweden," *Vigilantism against Migrants and Minorities*, Tore Bjørgå & Miroslav Mareš (eds), Routledge, 2019.

Gardell, Mattias, "'The Girl Who Was Chased by Fire': Violence and Passion in Contemporary Swedish Fascist Fiction," *Fascism: Journal of Comparative Fascism Studies*, 10:1, 2021.

Gardell, Mattias, Heléne Lööw, & Mikael Dahlberg-Grundberg, *Den ensamme terroristen*, Ordfront, 2017.

Gaposchkin, M. Cecilia, *Invisible Weapons: Liturgy and the Making of Crusade Ideology*, Cornell University Press, 2017.

Gill, Paul, John Horgan, & Paige Deckert, *Tracing the Motivations and Antecedent Behaviors of Lone-Actor Terrorism*, International Center for the Study of Terrorism, 2012.

Gill, Paul, John Horgan, & Paige Deckert, "Bombing Alone: Tracing the Motivations and Antecedent Behaviors of Lone-Actor Terrorists," *Journal of Forensic Science*, 59:2, 2014.

Gill, Paul, *Lone-Actor Terrorists: A Behavioural Analysis*, Routledge, 2016.

Grant, Madison, *The Passing of the Great Race*, Charles Scribner's Sons, 1916.

Greene, Viveca S., "'Deplorable' Satire: Alt-Right Memes, White Genocide Tweets, and Redpilling Normies," *Studies in American Humor*, 5:1, 2019.

Griffin, Roger, *The Nature of Fascism*, Pinter, 1992.

Griffin, Roger, *A Fascist Century*, ed. Matthew Feldman, Palgrave, 2008.

Griffin, Roger, "Lingua Quarti Imerii: The Euphemistic Tradition of the Extreme Right," *Doublespeak. The Rhetoric of the Far Right since 1945*, Mattehw Feldman & Paul Jackson (eds), ibidem-Verlag, 2014.

Griffin, Roger, "Studying Fascism in a Post-Fascist Age," *Fascism: Journal of Comparative Fascism Studies*, 6:1, 2017.

Griffin, Roger, *Fascism*, Polity, 2018.

Grundström, Karin & Irene Molina, "From Folkhem to Lifestyle Housing in Sweden: Segregation and Urban Form, 1930s–2010s," *International Journal of Housing Policy*, 16:3, 2016.

Hamm, Mark S. & Ramón Spaaij, *The Age of Lone Wolf Terrorism*, Columbia University Press, 2017.

Halder, Generaloberst Franz, *Kriegstagebuch*, ed. Hans-Adolf Jacobsen, vol. II, 1963.

Hardt, Michael & Antoni Negri, *Empire*, Harvard University Press, 2001.

Hardt, Michael & Antoni Negri, *Multitude: War and Democracy in the Age of Empire*, Penguin, 2005.

Hill, Paul J., *Mix My Blood with the Blood of the Unborn*, Army of God, 2003.

Hillgruber, Andreas, "War in the East and the Extermination of the Jews," *The Nazi Holocaust, 3:1, The 'Final Solution'*, Robert Marrus (ed.), Mecler, 1989.

Hitler, Adolf, *Mein Kampf*, transl. James Murphy, Coda Books, 1939.

Hogstedt, Carl, Christer Hogstedt, Bernt Lundgren, & Henrik Moberg, *Hälsan på spåret*, Folkhälsoinstitutet, 2006.

Holland, Derek, Roberto Fiore, & Nick Griffin, *Winds of Change, Notes for the Reconquista*, Logik förlag, 2016.

Hood, Gregory, "Superman and the White Christ," *Dark Right: Batman Viewed from the Right*, Greg Johnson & Gregory Hood (eds), Counter-Currents, 2018.

Horseman, Reginald, *Race and Manifest Destiny*, Harvard University Press, 1981.

Horswell, Mike & Akil N. Awan (eds), *The Crusades in the Modern World*, Routledge, 2020.

Hoskins, Richard K., *Vigilantes of Christendom: The History of the Phineas Priesthood*, The Virginia Publishing Company, 1990.

How to Survive in the West: A Mujahid Guide, 2015.

Hultgren, Johan, *Border Walls Gone Green: Nature and Anti-immigrant Politics in America*, University of Minnesota Press, 2015.

"Inspire Reactions," *Inspire*, no. 4, 2015.

Jacobson, Matthew Frey, *Whiteness of a Different Color*, Harvard University Press, 1998.

Jenkins, Brian Michael, *Stray Dogs and Virtual Armies: Radicalization and Recruitment to Jihadist Terrorism in the United States Since 9/11*, RAND Corporation, 2011.

Jensen, Richard Bach, "The Pre-1914 Anarchist 'Lone Wolf' Terrorist and Governmental Responses," *Terrorism and Political Violence*, 26:1, 2014.

Jensen, Richard Bach, *The Battle against Anarchist Terrorism: An International History, 1878-1934*, Cambridge University, 2015.

Johnson, Greg, "Superheroes, Sovereignty, and the Deep State," *Dark Right: Batman Viewed from the Right*, Greg Johnson & Gregory Hood (eds), Counter-Currents, 2018.

Johnson, Greg & Gregory Hood, "Why Are You People Here?" *Dark Right: Batman Viewed from the Right*, Greg Johnson & Gregory Hood (eds), Counter-Currents, 2018.

Jorjani, Jason, "Gotham Guardian: Will the Real Batman Please Stand Up," *Dark Right: Batman Viewed from the Right*, Greg Johnson & Gregory Hood (eds), Counter-Currents, 2018.

Kakel, Carol, *The American West and the Nazi East*, Macmillan, 2011.

Kamali, Sara, *Homegrown Hate*, University of California Press, 2021.

Kaplan, Jeffrey, "Leaderless Resistance," *Terrorism and Political Violence*, 9:3, 1997a.

Kaplan, Jeffrey, *Radical Religion in America*, Syracuse University Press, 1997b.

Kaplan, Jeffrey, "No Longer Alone: Lone Wolves, Wolf Packs and Made for Web TV Specials," *Far-Right Extremism in North America*, Barbara Perry, Jeff Gruenwald, & Ryan Scrivens (eds), Palgrave, forthcoming.

Kaplan, Jeffrey & Leonard Weinberg, *The Emergence of a Euro-American Radical Right*, Rutgers University Group, 1998.

King, Miriam & Steven Ruggles, "American Immigration, Fertility, and Race Suicide at the Turn of the Century," *Journal of Interdisciplinary History*, 20:3, 1990.

Kühl, Stefan, *The Nazi Connection: Eugenics, American Racism, and German National Socialism*, Oxford University Press, 2012.

Lane, David, *Revolution by the Number 14*, 14 Word Press, 1994a.

Lane, David, *The Auto-Biographical Portrait of the Life of David Lane and the 14 Word Motto*, 14 Word Press, 1994b.

Lane, David, *White Genocide Manifesto*, 14 Word Press, 1994c.

Lane, David, "The Price of Continued Reality Denial," *Focus Fourteen*, no. 507, 1995a.

Lane, David, "The Former Yugoslavia and the New World Order," *Focus Fourteen*, no. 603, 1995b.

Lane, David, "Now or Never...," *Focus Fourteen*, no. 609, 1996.

Lane, David, *Deceived, Damned and Defiant: The Revolutionary Writings of David Lane*, 14 Word Press, 1997.

Lee, Robert G. & Sabine Wilke, "Forest as Volk," *Journal of Social and Ecological Boundaries*, 1:1, 2015.

Lekan, Tomas, "Regionalism and the Politics of Landscape Preservation in the Third Reich," *Environmental History*, 4:3, 1999.

Linkola, Pentti, *Can Life Prevail?*, Artkos, 2011.

Lone Mujahid Pocketbook, al-Qaida in the Arabian Peninsula, Spring 1434, 2013.

López, Ian Haney, *White by Law*, New York University Press, 2006.

Lorenz, Taylor, "The Shooter's Manifesto Was Designed to Troll," *The Atlantic, Technology*, March 15, 2019.

Lutton, Wayne & John Tanton, *The Immigration Invasion*, The Social Contract, 1994.

Lynch, Trevor, *White Nationalist Guide to the Movies*, Counter-Currents, 2013.

Lynch, Trevor, "Man of Steel," *Dark Right: Batman Viewed from the Right*, Greg Johnson & Gregory Hood (eds), Counter-Currents, 2018.

Lynch, Trevor, "Batman vs Superman," *Dark Right: Batman Viewed from the Right*, Greg Johnson & Gregory Hood (eds), Counter-Currents, 2018.

Macdonald, Andrew [William Pierce], *Turner Diaries*, 2nd edn, National Vanguard Books, 1980 [1978].

Macdonald, Andrew [William Pierce], *Hunter*, 2nd edn, National Vanguard Books, 1989.

Macklin, Graham, "Teaching the Truth to the Hardcore," *Doublespeak: The Rhetoric of the Far Right Since 1945*, Matthew Feeldman & Paul Jackson (eds), ibidem-Verlag, 2014.

Mangan, J.A., *Shaping the Superman: Fascist Body as Political Icon – Aryan Fascism*, Frank Cass, 1999.

Markowski, Michael, "Crucesignatus: Its Origins and Early Usage," *Journal of Medieval History*, 10:3, 1984.

Mason, James, "Removing All Options," *Siege*, IX:4, 1980a.

Mason, James, "The N.S.L.F. and the Move Towards Revolution Through Armed Struggle," *Siege*, IX:4, 1980b.

Mason, James, "Strength and Spirit," *Siege*, IX:6, 1980c.

Mason, James, "An American Revolutionary Hero," *Siege*, 1981a.

Mason, James, "Playing the Ball as it Lies," *Siege*, 1981b.

Mason, James, "The NSLF One-Man Army," *Siege*, X:1, 1981c.

Mason, James, "Strike Hard, Strike Deep," *Siege*, X:2, 1981d.

Mason, James, "In Reverse," *Siege*, XIV:9, 1985.

Mason, James, "Charles Manson," *Siege*, XV:5, 1986.

Mason, James, "Integral Part of The Problem," *Siege: The Collected Writings of James Mason*, Michael Jenkins [Mihcael Moynihan] (ed.), Storm Books, 1992a.

Mason, James, "Of Pigs and Professionals," *Siege: The Collected Writings of James Mason*, Michael Jenkins [Mihcael Moynihan] (ed.),Storm Books, 1992b.

Mason, James, "Revolution in Reality," *Siege: The Collected Writings of James Mason*, Michael Jenkins [Mihcael Moynihan] (ed.),Storm Books, 1992c.

Mason, James, "The Mathematics of Terror," *Siege: The Collected Writings of James Mason*, Michael Jenkins [Mihcael Moynihan] (ed.),Storm Books, 1992d.

Mason, James, "Viking Berserker Rage," *Siege: The Collected Writings of James Mason*, Michael Jenkins [Mihcael Moynihan] (ed.),Storm Books, 1992e.

May, Rob & Matthew Feldman, "Understanding the Alt-Right: Ideologues, 'Lulz' and Hiding in Plain Sight," *Post-Digital Cultures of the Far Right*, Maik Fielitz & Nick Thurston (eds), transcript Verlag, 2019.

McAuley, James, "How Gay Icon Renaud Camus Became the Ideologue of White Supremacy," *The Nation*, June 17, 2019.

McFarland, Michael & Glenn Gottfried, "The Chosen Ones: A Mythic Analysis of the Theological and Political Self-Justification of Christian Identity," *Journal for the Study of Religion*, 15;1, 2002.

Metzger, Tom, "Laws of the Lone Wolf," *Stormfront*, May 13, 2010.

Metzger, Tom, "Joseph Tommasi Tribute," *Stormfront*, n.d.

Metzger, Tom, "Mini Manual for Survival," *The Insurgent*, n.d.

Metzger, Tom, "White Aryan Resistance Positions," *WAR Declared!*, n.d.

Michael, George, *Lone Wolf Terror and the Rise of Leaderless Resistance*, Vanderbildt University Press, 2012.

Michael, George, "This is War! Tom Metzger, White Aryan Resistance, and the Lone Wolf Legacy", *Focus on Terrorism*, XIV, 2016.

Mitchell, Ciara, Tweet, "Svar till @fbnewsroom", March 17, https:// twitter.com/fbnewsroom/status/1107117981358682112, 2019.

Mudde, Cas, *On Extremism and Democracy in Europe*, Routledge, 2016.

"New Zealand's Tech Community Mourns the Loss of Two Members in the Christchurch Shooting," Idealog Tech, March 18, https://idealog.co.nz/tech/2019/03/new-zealands-tech-community-mourns-loss-two-members-christchurch-terror-attack, 2019.

Nilsson, Per-Erik, *Open Source Jihad: Problematizing the Academic Discourse on Islamic Terrorism in Contemporary Europe*, Cambridge University Press, 2018.

Nilsson, Per-Erik, "'Give. Them. Hell' Conspirational Racialization and Anthropoemic Populism in Self-Acclaimed Ethno-Soldiers' Manifestos," *Critical Research on Religion*, forthcoming, 2021.

"Norway Sentences Oslo Mosque Shooter to 21 Years in Prison," Al Jazeera, June 11, 2020.

NSLF, *Political Terror*, National Socialist Liberation Front, 1974.

NSM Michigan, *A Brief History of American National Socialism*, n.d.

OECD, *Income Inequality Data Update: Sweden*, Organisation for Economic Co-operation and Development, 2015.

Orbach, Danny, "Tyrannicide in Radical Islam," *Middle Eastern Studies*, 48:6, 2012.

P4 Malmö, "Misstänkt skottlossning utanför barnakuten," *P4 Malmöhus*, September 26, 2010.

Pantucci, Raffaello, "A Typology of Lone Wolves: Preliminary Analysis of Lone Islamist Terrorists," *Developments in Radicalisation and Political Violence*, Harvey Rubin & John Bew (eds), International Centre for the Study of Radicalisation and Political Violence, 2011.

Powell, Enoch, *Freedom and Reality*, Elliot Right Way Books, 1969.

Raspail, Jean, *Le Camp des Saints*, Editions Robert Laffont, 1973.

Ray, Zachary O., "The Alt Knight," *Dark Right: Batman Viewed from the Right*, Greg Johnson & Gregory Hood (eds), Counter-Currents, 2018.

Regal, Brian, "Madison Grant, Maxwell Perkins, and Eugenics Publishing at Scribner's," *Princeton University Library Chronicle*, 65:2, 2004.

RNZCGP, "New Medal Honours Dr Amjad Hamid, Killed in Christchurch Mosque Attack," Media Release, *New Zealand Doctor*, March 10, www .nzdoctor.co.nz/article/undoctored/new-medal-honours-dr-amjad-hamid-killed-christchurch-mosque-attack, 2020.

Rohe, John F., *Mary Lou & John Tanton: A Journey into American Conservation*, FAIR Horizon Press, 2002.

Rosenberg, Alfred, *The Myth of the Twentieth Century*, Ostara Publications, 1939.

Rudolph, Eric, *Between the Lines of Drift: The Memoirs of a Militant*, Army of God, 2013.

Ryback, Timothy W., *Hitler's Private Library*, Vintage, 2010.

Rydgren, Jens, "Introduction," *The Oxford Handbook of the Radical Right*, Jens Rydgren (ed.), Oxford Handbooks Online, 2018.

Schama, Simon, *Landscape and Memory*, Vintage, 1996.

Schuurman, Bart, Lars Lindekilde, Stefan Malthaner, Francis O'Connor, Paul Gill, & Noémie Bouhana, "End of the Lone Wolf: The Typology that Should Not Have Been," *Studies in Conflict & Terrorism*, 42:8, 2019.

Silva, Tiago João Queimada, "The Reconquista Revisited," *The Crusades in the Modern World*, Mike Horswell & Akil N. Awan (eds), Routledge, 2020.

Simmons, Bill, "13 White Supremacists Acquitted in Arkansas Murder and Sedition Trial," *The Washington Post*, April 8, 1988.

Smith, Woodruff D., "Friedrich Ratzel and the Origins of Lebensraum," *German Studies Review*, 3:1, 1980.

Spiro, Jonathan Peter, *Defending the Master Race: Conservation, Eugenics, and the Legacy of Madison Grant*, University of Vermont Press, 2009.

Stephens, Piers, "Blood, Not Soil: Anna Bramwell and the Myth of 'Hitler's Green Party'," *Organization & Environment*; 14:2, 2001.

Stern, Jessica, "The Covenant, the Sword, and the Arm of the Lord," Toxic Terror, Jonathan Tucker (ed.), The MIT Press, 2000.

Spaaij, Ramón, *Understanding Lone Wolf Terrorism*, Springer, 2012.

Spackman, Barbara, *Fascist Virilities. Rhetoric, Ideology, and Social Fantasy in Italy*, University of Minnesota Press, 1996.

Staudenmaier, Peter, "Fascist Ecology: The 'Green Wing' of the Nazi Party and its Historical Antecedents," *The Pomegranate: Journal of Pagan Studies*, 15, 2001.

Staudenmaier, Peter, "Organic Farming in Nazi Germany: The Politics of Biodynamic Agriculture, 1933–1945," *Environmental History*, 18:2, 2013.

Stoddard, Lothrop, *The Rising Tide of Color*, Charles Scribner's Sons, 1920.

Stoddard, Lothrop, *The Revolt Against Civilization: The Menace of the Under-Man*, Charles Scribner's Sons, 1922.

Taylor, Jared, "Race Realism," *A Fair Hearing: The Alt-Right in the Words of Its Members and Leaders*, George T. Shaw (ed.), Arktos, 2018.

Teich, Sarah, *Trends and Developments in Lone Wolf Terrorism in the Western World: An Analysis of Terrorist Attacks and Attempted Attacks by Islamic Extremists*, Institute for Counter-Terrorism, 2013.

"To the Knights of the Lone Jihad," *Inspire*, no. 10, Spring 1434, 2013.

Tommasi, Joseph, *Strategy for Revolution*, National Socialist Liberation Front, c. 1974a.

Tommasi, Joseph, *Building the Revolutionary Party*, National Socialist Liberation Front, c. 1974b.

"Transcript of Dred Scott v. Sanford" (1857), *Our Documents*, www.ourdocuments.gov/doc.php?flash=false&doc=29&page=transcript.

Warthan, Perry, "Terrorism," *Universal Order*, Supplement, *Siege*, n.d.

"Wilāyat Ar-Raqqah – Ramadān 26," *Dabiq*, Ramadan 1435, 2014.

Whitman, James Q., *Hitler's American Model*, Princeton University Press, 2017.

Windsor, Will, "A Dark Knight Without A King," *Dark Right: Batman Viewed from the Right*, Greg Johnson & Gregory Hood (eds), Counter-Currents, 2018.

Zimmerman, Michael E. & Teresa A. Toulouse, "Ecofascism," *Keywords for Environmental Studies*, Joni Adamson, William A. Gleason, & David N. Pellow (eds), New York University Press, 2016.

Acknowledgments

This study is part of the project "Angry white men? A study of violent racism, correlations between organized and unorganized hate crime and the affective dimensions of ultranationalism," financed by the Swedish Research Council (2016-04758). I would first like to express my sincere gratitude to the scholars and friends who were part of that project, Simon Lindgren, Samuel Merrill, Mathilda Åkerlund, and Heléne Lööw, for intellectually rewarding discussions about such a troublesome theme as white racist lone wolf serial killers and mass murderers. My colleagues at the Centre for Multidisciplinary Studies of Racism at Uppsala University have as always provided an amazingly creative and rich research environment that greatly has contributed to sharpening the analysis of the study, as have my fellow Fascism Studies colleagues in the Network for Nordic Fascism Studies, NORFAS, Terje Emberland, Nicola Karcher, Oula Silvennoinen, Leena Malkki, Daniel Sallamaa, Tommi Kotonen, Claus Bundgård Christensen, Lars M. Andersson, Markus Lundström, and Heléne Lööw. A very special thank you goes out to Jeffrey Kaplan, one of the first scholars to observe and take seriously the shift in white racist violent tactics that became leaderless resistance, for his immensely valuable reading and constructive criticism of the full manuscript, and to Anthony Fiscella for questioning the very grounds of the project as such, which in different ways made me rethink my arguments and return to the political landscape under investigation to make sure that no stone was left unturned. Throughout the project, the Cambridge Elements in Religion and Violence editors James R. Lewis and Margo Kitts have been consistently encouraging, and reinjected energy into the project at precisely the right time to make it happen. The precision and exactitude of the Element's copy-editor Dan Shutt has been especially appreciated. Any remaining errors are, of course, mine. Had it not been for the love and affection of my wonderful children and the ever-expanding number of fantastic grandchildren, this project would never have been possible. Linus, Emma, Moa, Ida, Sofia, Stefan, Kim,

Alaska, Nikkie, and Norma; Maya, Amira, Saga, Theo, Yasin, Amir, Ayleen, Aiden, and Amelia: you are my love, my joy, my life. Finally, my wife and partner in the adventure of life and love has, as always, also been my first reader, my sharpest critic, and my intellectual discussant. Edda Manga, this is for you.

About the Author

Mattias Gardell is Nathan Söderblom Professor in Comparative Religion and Director of Research at the Centre for Multidisciplinary Studies of Racism, Uppsala University.

Cambridge Elements ≡

Religion and Violence

James R. Lewis
Wuhan University

James R. Lewis is Professor at Wuhan University, and the author and editor of a number of volumes, including *The Cambridge Companion to Religion and Terrorism*.

Margo Kitts
Hawai'i Pacific University

Margo Kitts edits the *Journal of Religion and Violence* and is Professor and Coordinator of Religious Studies and East-West Classical Studies at Hawai'i Pacific University in Honolulu.

ABOUT THE SERIES

Violence motivated by religious beliefs has become all too common in the years since the 9/11 attacks. Not surprisingly, interest in the topic of religion and violence has grown substantially since then. This Elements series on Religion and Violence addresses this new, frontier topic in a series of ca. fifty individual Elements. Collectively, the volumes will examine a range of topics, including violence in major world religious traditions, theories of religion and violence, holy war, witch hunting, and human sacrifice, among others.

Cambridge Elements ☰

Religion and Violence

A full series listing is available at: www.cambridge.org/ERAV

Printed in the United States
by Baker & Taylor Publisher Services

Printed in the United States
by Baker & Taylor Publisher Services